Teaching in a Nutshell

D0165778

Designed to help student teachers develop an *approach* to teaching that is both theoretical and practical, this text focuses on key aspects of teaching rather than trying to "cover the waterfront." Based on extensive research on teachers' views, their own long experience as teacher educators, and other sources, the authors recommend seven priorities for teaching and teacher education:

- program planning
- pupil assessment
- classroom organization and community
- inclusive education
- subject content and pedagogy
- professional identity
- a vision for teaching

Each chapter deals in turn with one of these priorities, using a common format. *Activities* throughout help readers understand what the priority means in both theory and practice.

This text is a companion to the authors' 2009 book for teacher educators, *Priorities in Teacher Education: The 7 Key Elements of Pre-Service Preparation.* By making these seven priorities and related knowledge explicit, it helps student teachers to acquire essential knowledge and skills, to understand the teaching/learning process more fully, and above all to be as prepared as possible for the demanding work of teaching.

Clare Kosnik is Professor, Department of Curriculum, Teaching & Learning, Ontario Institute for Studies in Education/University of Toronto.

Clive Beck is Professor, Centre for Teacher Development, Ontario Institute for Studies in Education/University of Toronto.

Teaching in a Nutshell

Navigating Your Teacher Education Program as a Student Teacher

Clare Kosnik and Clive Beck

Routledge
Taylor & Francis Group

NEW YORK AND LONDON

First published 2011
by Routledge
270 Madison Avenue, New York, NY 10016

Simultaneously published in the UK
by Routledge
2 Park Square, Milton Park, Abingdon, Oxon OX14 4RN

Routledge is an imprint of the Taylor & Francis Group, an informa business

© 2011 Taylor & Francis

The right of Clare Kosnik and Clive Beck to be identified as
authors of this work has been asserted by them in accordance
with sections 77 and 78 of the Copyright, Designs and Patents
Act 1988.

Typeset in Sabon by Wearset Ltd, Boldon, Tyne and Wear
Printed and bound in the United States of America on acid-
free paper by Walsworth Publishing Company, Marceline, MO.

Library of Congress Cataloging in Publication Data
Kosnik, Clare Madott.
Teaching in a nutshell: navigating your teacher education
program as a student teacher/by Clare Kosnik and Clive Beck.
p. cm.
Includes bibliographical references.
1. Student teaching. 2. Teachers—Training of. I. Beck, Clive. II.
Title.
LB2157.A3K67 2011
370.71'1–dc22   2010032934

ISBN13: 978-0-415-88806-6 (hbk)
ISBN13: 978-0-415-88807-3 (pbk)
ISBN13: 978-0-203-83269-1 (ebk)

To the new teachers who participated in the study on which this text is based, welcoming us into their classrooms year after year, generously giving time for interviews, and offering thoughtful comments about teaching and teacher education. And to our own pre-service students who have discussed the emerging findings in classes and helped us refine our approach to teacher education.

Contents

Acknowledgments

As noted in the dedication, we are very grateful to the new teachers whose experiences, views, and practices have contributed enormously to this text, and to the many pre-service students with whom we have discussed the findings and implications of the research. We also wish to thank our research team for their unfailing commitment to the project, their sensitivity and skill in interacting with the new teachers, and their invaluable input and guidance. We acknowledge, too, the strong support of our faculty colleagues in our research, writing, and teaching, and offer special thanks to Frances Tolnai, whose able transcribing of interviews continues to be crucial to our work. Finally, we wish to thank the Social Sciences and Humanities Research Council of Canada for its generous funding of the research.

Introduction

Becoming a teacher is hard work! *Being* a teacher is hard work! Yet teaching can be highly rewarding and stimulating work. In most countries, the government requires individuals to complete a teacher education program before assuming full responsibility of a class. You have enrolled in such a "pre-service" program. Our goal in this book is to help you get the most out of your teacher education program.

Teacher education programs are not all the same in either content or format. For example, the length of programs varies widely: 10 months; 12 months; two-year post-undergraduate degree; combined study of liberal arts courses (e.g., English literature, history, psychology) and teacher education, often over four years; a short "alternative certification" program of a couple of months; or a combined work-study program. The program that you selected may be at a nationally renowned institution or your local university or college. Regardless of the length, structure, or content of your program, you will find many surprises in becoming a teacher.

Having worked in teacher education for many years, we know that student teachers (or "teacher candidates" as they are sometimes called) often find the program intense. There are many courses, activities, practicum placements (in schools, daycare, community centers), and assignments; this combination of academic study and practicum work can make your program hectic. Time management and juggling competing demands can pose real challenges. Being well organized is essential.

Further complicating the process is the fact that sometimes you will feel like a student and at other times like a full-fledged teacher. This shifting of identity from student to teacher and back again is something that our student teachers have told us creates unease. Try to enjoy being a student as well as a teacher, because this may be the last time you have such support for your work.

An additional stress in the process of becoming a teacher is that instructors vary in the theories or teaching strategies they say are essential, critically important, the linchpin of the program. This can result in becoming overwhelmed and getting lost trying to figure out what is actually important at this stage of your development. In our research we have heard beginning teachers say that the program overwhelmed them, that it became "a blur" because it was so busy and fast-paced, and everything was deemed critically important. This is unfortunate because becoming a teacher requires having clear goals and a beginning repertoire of key skills and knowledge. Without this, your work as a beginning teacher can be exceedingly difficult. If you feel overwhelmed, take a step back, take a deep breath, figure out what most needs to be done, and then proceed with an approach and a plan.

What you most need to learn as a student teacher differs from one person to another: some of you may have taught English in Asia for a few years, some may have been educational assistants, some may have come to teacher education with little experience working in schools. Becoming a teacher is not a one-size-fits-all undertaking. Further, becoming a teacher does not happen once-for-all: your development as a teacher will continue for the rest of your career. The pre-service program is only one step in a continuum of teacher education: there is always much more to learn. That is partly why teaching is such a rewarding profession: we never stop learning.

Why did we write this book? Briefly put, we want to help you navigate your pre-service teacher education program. In a sense, student teachers and new teachers today receive a great deal of direction on what and how to teach. Their pre-service instructors offer them a wide array of theories, principles, and strategies, and their practicum mentors give them plenty of practical advice. After graduating, they are often handed detailed curriculum guidelines, prescribed or recommended teaching materials, and mandated assessment and reporting systems. Further guidance usually comes from their school principal, experienced colleagues, and school district and government induction programs. At a less formal level, teachers are also aware of the views of parents, politicians, and the public at large about how they should do their job. Yet all this information and advice may be too much! It may in fact leave you without a clear sense of direction. Why is this?

- In teacher education programs, faculty often try to do too much. We try to cover the waterfront in almost every subject and end up overwhelming students.
- Student teachers are inundated with so much information they have a difficult time organizing it both conceptually and physically.
- Student teachers need some guidance on how to capitalize on their teacher education program. Often what they think they need or want may not in fact be what is most beneficial for them at this point in time. (The new teachers in our study – described below – in

a way can be your mentors, telling you what is really important for you to learn, what to focus on in the two components of your pre-service program: the course work and practice teaching.)

- Teacher educators need to be explicit about priorities and connections, not leaving so much for student teachers and beginning teachers to figure out on their own. We also need to be realistic about what can and should be taught during teacher education. Not that we should impose an approach to teaching on student teachers, but we must work *with* them in figuring out what takes precedence and how the pieces fit together.

Sharing the Secrets with Student Teachers

There has been a dramatic increase in research on teacher education – on teacher educators, student teachers, program structure, and the content of courses. This research is helping teacher educators determine how best to support student teachers. We believe that sharing the insights researchers have gained with you who are becoming teachers should be an integral part of the pre-service curriculum. The research findings should not be a secret that only teacher educators possess: student teachers also need to have access to this knowledge. In this section, we present a few findings that illustrate how knowledge of research can help you understand more fully the process of becoming a teacher.

From our experience, student teachers are extremely keen. You go into teaching because you want to make a difference and because you enjoy the teaching process and working with children and youth. This is wonderful because we need committed teachers; however, the reality of teaching often overwhelms young teachers. We feel that becoming aware of the following three challenges will help you acquire insight into the process of becoming a teacher. Prominent researcher Linda Darling-Hammond, in her book *Powerful Teacher Education: Lessons from Exemplary Programs* (2006), identifies three major challenges new teachers face.

Apprenticeship of Observation

You have been a student for many years; it is estimated that high school graduates have spent over 13,000 hours in school. Accordingly, you have already had many opportunities to observe *teaching in action*. This has given you many ideas about teaching and familiarity with the setting in which you will work. These hours of observation were important; however, they were of restricted value because you always saw teaching from a student's perspective. Dan Lortie is another world-renowned researcher who studied teachers closely. In his book, *Schoolteacher: A Sociological Study* (1975), he coined the phrase "apprenticeship of observation" to describe the extensive experience you have had as a student. He also outlined some of the limitations of this apprenticeship.

- You only saw teaching from a student's perspective.
- You were not privy to the decision-making role of the teacher.
- You could not debrief with the teacher after the lesson to discuss what worked and what did not.
- You could not "see" the emotional aspect of teaching, the range of emotions teachers experience.
- You were often unaware of the amount of time your teachers spent preparing lessons, marking assignments, and preparing report cards.
- You did not witness the many other tasks teachers must perform (e.g., staff meetings, meetings with parents, meetings with colleagues, in-service sessions).

As a result of this apprenticeship of observation, you have a skewed vision of teaching, one that only tells part of the story. From our work with new teachers, we have learned that they are often surprised by the extensive decision-making role of the teacher, the emotional aspect of teaching, and the sheer volume of work. Through this text, we want to help you become prepared for the key tasks and responsibilities that comprise the work of a teacher.

Challenge of Enactment

In your university courses you are presented with many interesting suggestions for lessons, and you develop many ideas on how you want your class to work (e.g., layout of the classroom, the way you interact with your pupils). But putting these ideas into action is often difficult. The problem is one of *enactment*. Going from ideas to actually doing the lesson with a class of 20 to 35 students who have a range of abilities and interests – in a classroom that may not have an ideal physical set-up – is often not an easy task. Darling-Hammond (2006) describes the problem of enactment as follows:

> Teachers-in-training must not only understand how people learn and what teaching strategies may help them; they must also learn to present information clearly, lead discussions that really get at the ideas under study, manage discourse of many kinds, organize groups for learning and give them useful tasks they can do, manage student behavior, weigh difficult dilemmas and make quick decisions, plan well and alter plans for unforeseen circumstances, respond to children, and respond to questions about the material they are teaching.
>
> (p. 37)

As you gain more teaching experience, you will learn to gauge the amount of material that can be covered in a lesson, focus on the big ideas of the lesson, estimate the attention span of your students (it varies from year to year), and balance teacher-directed lessons, whole-class discussion, small-group work, and individual work. It takes time to be able to determine what is realistic for individual students and the class as a whole. As this becomes "second-nature" to you, the problems of enactment will diminish dramatically. Give yourself time.

Challenge of Complexity

The third point on the triangle is *complexity*. As you begin to teach, you quickly realize that there is much more to teaching than simply delivering a well-planned lesson. Teaching is not a straightforward process, where the teacher teaches and all students learn. Teaching and learning occur in a dynamic environment where much is happening simultaneously. McDonald (1992) describes it as follows:

> Real teaching happens within a wild triangle of relations – among teacher, students, subject – and the points of this triangle shift continuously. What shall I teach amid all that I should teach? How can I grasp it myself so that my grasping might enable theirs? What are they thinking and feeling – toward me, toward each other, toward the thing I am trying to teach? How near should I come, how far off should I stay? How much clutch, how much gas?
>
> (p. 1)

As you gain experience, you will learn how to deal with the complexity of teaching more easily by acquiring a repertoire of strategies (for both teaching and classroom management) that reduce some of the surprises and challenges; however, the complexity never goes away. You simply get much better at dealing with all the permutations and issues involved.

We outline this triangle of challenges not to frighten you but to show the value of research on teaching and, most importantly, to help prepare you for the reality of teaching. We want to ensure that when you experience some of the dilemmas noted above, you have the comfort of knowing that all teachers experience them and you are not inadequate. Having challenges and responding to them in a thoughtful way is all part of being a teacher.

Priorities in Teacher Education

For the past six years we have been studying two groups of beginning teachers, some now in their sixth year of teaching and others in their third year. They are from a variety of teacher education programs (one-year, two-year, four-year concurrent) and teaching in two countries, Canada and the United States. Most are working in urban schools with a student population that is very diverse academically, racially, culturally, and socioeconomically. Over the years, we have observed them teach and interviewed them on a regular basis.

The goal of our research has been to pursue certain key questions about teacher education: What can student teachers learn during their teacher education program? What do beginning teachers need to know to survive and thrive in the busy early years of teaching? What should we actually be emphasizing in our teacher education program? Based on the new teachers' views and other sources, we have arrived at the following seven priorities for teacher education:

- program planning;
- pupil assessment;
- classroom organization and community;
- inclusive education;
- subject content and pedagogy;
- professional identity;
- a vision for teaching.

These priorities are described in detail in the seven chapters of this volume and in a companion book for teacher educators, *Priorities in Teacher Education: The 7 Key Elements of Pre-Service Preparation* (2009). We feel that by making the priorities explicit to student teachers in this text, we will help you capitalize on your teacher education program, acquire essential knowledge and skills, understand the teaching/learning process more fully, and above all be as prepared as possible for the demanding work of teaching. Most of the examples and quotations from new teachers included here are taken from the initial three years of our study.

As long-time teacher education instructors and researchers ourselves, we have drawn not only on the above study of new teachers but also our own experiences and observations in a variety of university and school settings. In fact, we have already "tried out" many of the ideas and activities in this text with student teachers in pre-service courses (and with experienced teachers in graduate courses), and their feedback has influenced our thinking considerably.

Terminology

As we said earlier, teacher education does not take a universal form and even the language varies widely. In this text, we will use terms as follows.

- *Academic program* refers to the courses you complete on the university or college campus. Some are in curriculum areas (often called methods or C&I courses) while others look at broader issues (often called foundations courses).

- Almost all teacher education programs have a block or blocks of time when student teachers are placed in a school, usually in a class with an experienced teacher. We refer to this as *practice teaching.* Some may know it as student teaching, or the practicum, while others may refer to it as an internship. The length of time for practice teaching varies widely from a two-week block in a school to a year-long placement where student teachers are in the academic program half the day and practice teaching the other half.

- The experienced teachers with whom student teachers are placed mentor them, give them feedback, usually assess them, and often share resources with them. These teachers may be called cooperating teachers, associate teachers, host teachers, mentor teachers, or teacher educators. Throughout this text, we refer to them as *cooperating teachers.*

- The university or college faculty – whether tenure-line or contract – who help supervise student teachers in their practice teaching placement also go by a variety of names. We refer to them here as *university supervisors.* Their primary responsibility is to support the student teachers and cooperating teachers; often they evaluate the student teachers.

- The students in a teacher education program are referred to variously as student teachers, teacher candidates, pre-service teachers, interns, or teachers-in-training. We prefer the term *student teachers* because it recognizes that you are a student learning to be a teacher.

Structure of the Book

Each chapter of the book deals with one of the seven priorities, using a common format. We begin the chapter with a discussion of the *what* and *why* of the priority in question, followed by *a case study* of a beginning teacher (a participant in our research) showing how he or she implements this priority. From there we outline some of the *challenges* of implementing the priority, and then describe *principles and strategies* for meeting these challenges.

Included throughout each chapter are *activities* to help you understand what the priority means in both theory and practice, which in turn will support your work as a student teacher and later a beginning teacher. These activities can be done on your own or with others. Below is a short description of the types of activities we have developed. You can use them as they are or modify them for your particular needs:

- *Personal activity*: These activities usually involve your thinking about the topic in relation to your work as a teacher or your experiences as a school student or student teacher.
- *Case study activity*: This involves reading the case study of the beginning teacher profiled in a particular chapter and considering the questions posed at the end, individually or as a group.
- *During the academic program*: These activities can be done as part of a curriculum methods course (e.g., literacy, mathematics, science) or a foundations course (e.g., school and society, philosophy of education, general pedagogy).
- *During practice teaching*: These can be done on your own or in consultation with your cooperating teacher.
- *Resource Kit*: This involves building your own collection of curriculum and classroom organization strategies, curriculum and professional resources, and curriculum tips (e.g., poems, chants, songs, bulletin board captions, classroom management ideas, photocopies of interesting lesson plans, samples of student work, photographs, or field trip guides). We have found that having student teachers start organizing their resources while in the pre-service program does just that – it organizes them and helps them devise a system upon which they can build. *Organize your Kit in a way that works for you!* For example, binders, computer disks, and file folders are useful tools. Store your materials in a banker's box, Rubbermaid storage container, milk carton plastic bin, or a series of binders. As you assemble your Resource Kit, be selective. It should not be simply a repository for all the handouts you receive in your university classes. Think of your Kit as a "resource" for you as a teacher.

We hope this text will help you navigate your teacher education program to become the best teacher you can be. Regardless of the length, structure, or content of your program, there will be highs and lows that are all part of the process. Keep your focus on your learning; be aware how political and contestable many aspects of education are; and be open-minded. Being a teacher is often not as it is portrayed in popular culture, nor is it exactly as you remember it from your own student days. Teaching is a complex activity that requires teachers to be very able and caring. And that is what we hope you will be. Best wishes for your studies.

Clare and Clive

Chapter 1

Program Planning

During your teacher education program, you most likely have learned how to write a lesson plan and develop a unit plan (for a particular curriculum topic). Both of these are essential skills for teaching but they only are part of the work you will do in planning the curriculum. The aspect of teaching emphasized most by the new teachers in our study was program planning – that is, creating an integrated, feasible set of educational experiences for a class across the whole year. Program planning is much more than just planning a lesson or unit. It involves deciding what to emphasize, figuring out how to link topics, and adapting lessons to the needs and abilities of the class. The scope of program planning took many of our teachers by surprise.

PERSONAL ACTIVITY

When you think about being a teacher, how do you conceptualize the role? To what extent do you see yourself as a decision-maker? Or did you think you would implement the formal curriculum in a fairly straightforward way?

Why is Program Planning Important?

Beginning teachers are often shocked at how little time they have for actual instruction. In practice teaching during the pre-service program they were given the time they needed to teach lessons; and they thought that, as full-time teachers, it would be like this throughout the year. But, in reality, the time you actually have is greatly reduced because classes are cancelled due to school events or classes are interrupted by taking attendance, managing behavior, building community, administering formal assessments, gathering information for the principal, and so on. Program planning is necessary, then, for the following reasons:

1. **Given the shortage of time, we cannot possibly cover all curriculum topics in significant depth.** We have to decide which topics to address and how much time to give to them. Recognizing the need for decision-making of this kind is a key insight into teaching.
2. **Some topics are more important than others** for given individuals and groups. No matter how much time we had, we would still have to tailor the program to the distinctive needs and abilities of our class.
3. **Learning is unpredictable.** It develops in unforeseen ways, again depending on the individual or group. Planning, then, is an ongoing process throughout the school year. Serena, in her first year of teaching, noted that she creates a lot of her own teaching materials because her students' learning "is so unpredictable.... A lot of stuff I make is very tailored to them ... knowing what they need." John said that sometimes he sets aside a planned lesson to address "real questions that real children are asking." "Teachable moments" have to be grasped as they arise.
4. **Student engagement is crucial to learning.** We must plan a program that is of interest and relevance to our students so that they will be more involved, be less disruptive in class, and learn in greater depth (Allington, 2006; Atwell, 1998).

The importance of program planning (and teacher decision-making) is emphasized in the educational literature. For example, according to Dewey (1938):

> [Teaching] requires thought and planning ahead. The educator is responsible for a knowledge of individuals and for a knowledge of subject-matter that will enable activities to be selected which lend themselves to social organization ... in which all individuals have an opportunity to contribute something.
>
> (p. 56)

Hagger and McIntyre (2006) state that "teaching expertise" lies in "very subtle judgments about what standards to set, what actions to take, and what combinations of goals can realistically be sought" (p. 33). And Darling-Hammond (2006) refers to teachers as "adaptive experts," commenting:

> Teaching ... requires sophisticated judgment about how and what students are learning, what gaps in their understanding need to be addressed, what experiences will allow them to connect to what they need to know, and what instructional adaptations can ensure that they reach common goals.
>
> (p. 10)

What is Program Planning?

Briefly put, the program planning role of teachers involves deciding:

- which topics to include and how much emphasis to place on each;
- how to teach the topics: what materials, strategies, activities, and approaches to use;
- at what point in the year to address the topics;
- to what extent and in what ways to integrate the various subjects, topics, and activities;
- to what extent and in what ways to pursue broader and deeper learning goals – e.g., love of learning, research skills, collaborative skills – that cut across topics, activities, and subjects.

In some countries, all the teachers of a particular grade on a given day are literally "on the same page" of the official curriculum, teaching the same content and using almost the same activities. Most of the planning is done for them, centrally. In the school contexts we have researched, however, the responsibility for planning the school day, week, and year lies largely with the teacher (Clayton, 2007; Darling-Hammond, 2006; Hagger & McIntyre, 2006; Kennedy, 2005; Sleeter, 2005). Although the official curriculum lists topics and expectations for each grade, teachers – in varying degrees – tailor these guidelines to their class. As you can see, program planning is much more than planning a curriculum unit.

Toward the end of their first year, the new teachers in our study were beginning to understand their planning and decision-making role. For example, in April of his first year, David said:

> I think I relied too heavily [earlier in the year] on the school district program. It was a security thing for me, to make sure I did what the district asked me to do.... [I would advise a beginning teacher to think] what do you want to achieve in language arts, what is your language program? If you have a good idea then integrate that with the district program.... Do yours first and then match it up with the other and don't be afraid to take a little leniency with it.

Similarly, Nina saw that she had to adapt her program to her students: "I tried to use [an] approach to reading instruction ... we learned in pre-service, and I think the theory behind it is fantastic, but in a class like mine I simply can't do it."

ACTIVITY: During the Academic Program

If you are preparing to be an elementary school teacher, select one subject that you most likely will teach. If you are preparing to be a secondary school teacher, for this activity focus on your main teaching subject. Working in groups, review the official curriculum guideline for your chosen subject.

- How would you describe it: very detailed; just a guideline; fairly vague?
- Discuss whether it is feasible for a teacher to teach all of the topics outlined in the document with the same degree of emphasis.
- Identify the topics you think are the most important and the ones that are less important.
- Which topics need to be taught earliest (e.g., at the beginning of the year)?
- If possible, look at a copy of a practicing teacher's long-range plan. (A long-range plan is usually a detailed description of the units/topics to be taught for the entire year with accompanying descriptions of teaching strategies, student assignments, and assessment methods.) What do you notice about it? Consider the level of detail, sequence of topics, areas of emphasis, structure of the plan, and references to a textbook(s). Are all topics explored in the same level of detail?

ACTIVITY: For Your Resource Kit

During your practice teaching placements ask your cooperating teachers about the long-range plan requirement in their schools. Copy their long-range plans and file them in your Resource Kit. Try to collect several long-range plans.

Tanya's Approach to Program Planning: A Case Study

As a third-year teacher, life is getting a lot easier. Life is getting a lot like life; I'm getting a life. I'm staying up until 9:00 o'clock at night, which is a huge feat for me because in my first year it was 7:30 and I was falling asleep at the table.

Tanya, a new teacher in her mid-twenties, graduated in 2004 from a two-year master's credential program, specializing in kindergarten through grade 6. Her first three years of teaching, although they went relatively smoothly, were in three different grades – 1, 4, and 3 – in two different schools. The schools, both in the same district, were suburban and fairly affluent. They had a high proportion of minority students from South-East Asia and the Middle East, and several English Language Learners. During the master's program, Tanya had done three of her four practice teaching placements in the school where she was first hired to teach. She felt the extended time in the school was an apprenticeship of sorts. Her cooperating teachers had been outstanding practitioners and mentors for her.

Tanya's previous undergraduate degree was a Bachelor of Science in child studies. While not giving her a teaching credential, this small, prestigious program had a teacher preparation component, thus allowing her to begin learning the skills of program planning early in her studies. In the third year of this degree, Tanya had two practicum placements, one in a daycare center and one in senior kindergarten. In the fourth year, she did a semester-long placement (five days a week) in a grade 2 class, where she could observe and participate in the development and implementation of curriculum units. She thoroughly enjoyed the child studies degree because she acquired a deep understanding of child development, had extended experience working with children, learned skills of curriculum development, and honed her reflective practice skills. During the program, Tanya worked for three summers in a highly progressive daycare center emphasizing inquiry-based learning for both children and staff: the influence of this experience is evident in her current approach to program planning.

Tanya was very pleased with the master's credential program that followed because it provided further opportunities to learn planning and teaching skills while also addressing many theoretical concepts. The literacy courses in particular "gave us the philosophy we needed to make our way through our first year." She elaborated:

> If you come into teaching with the philosophy you want, then the other stuff will follow and you'll figure out how to fit your school's resources into your philosophy. If you have a strong philosophy – like fostering love of reading – that you're just not willing to let go, then you'll figure out the rest.

She recalled that the program also exposed her to a variety of resource materials that helped her in her planning as a beginning teacher.

Description of Practice

We consider Tanya's program planning in literacy to be exceptionally strong, especially for a new teacher. Now teaching grade 3, she uses a variety of excellent books of various genres; the reading materials are developmentally appropriate; she links reading and writing; spends time getting to know her students and carefully tracking their progress; she is highly focused on pupil learning, while recognizing however that children have to be motivated to read and write; she uses oral language as a bridge to print; she integrates literacy skills into the content areas; students read and write for extended periods each day; decoding and comprehension skills are taught both separately and in content-area lessons; and she uses many different teaching techniques (e.g., Readers Theatre, mini-chalk boards, literacy centers, and individual word processing).

Tanya's skills in program planning evolved over her first three years of teaching, but she was already quite able in her first year. She began in the same school and at the same grade level (grade 1) as in her final master's practicum, with a mentor teacher whose style and philosophy closely matched hers; accordingly, she was able to base her program on the one she had experienced. The mentor teacher did not rely heavily on a formal reading program; rather, she carefully selected texts and lessons from a range of sources. Tanya continued this thoughtful approach to planning, shunning the basal readers in favor of high quality children's literature and drawing on research to select specific decoding and comprehension skills to teach. By the end of her third year, she was able to report that "my kids are happy. And I feel pretty confident that they feel okay in here. They're willing to take risks, they're learning, they're progressing, and I'm confident they'll do okay next year."

No doubt Tanya's outstanding practicums helped prepare her for the difficult task of program planning; however, this only tells part of the story. As a beginning teacher, Tanya had a clear vision for her literacy program. Toward the end of her first year, she said:

> I want the children to become motivated to read and write. I want them to work in a group so they can talk about reading and writing and actually do it, responding to books through writing or more reading, or manipulating something or listening to something rather than answering a question on a worksheet.

Her vision helped guide her selection of topics and tasks; however, she faced programming challenges in her first year, including "knowing how much work to put in front of the students to keep their attention … knowing what to teach them and when to teach them and how to teach them." As time passed and she got to know her students better, these challenges decreased significantly.

In each of her first three years, Tanya was keen to co-plan with her grade partners, but she had limited success due to timetabling logistics, conflicting philosophies, and other factors. When teaching grade 4 (in her second year), she and another new teacher co-planned many of their lessons and units, and she found this very rewarding and useful:

> We bounce ideas off each other, we have the same books for our literature circles or sometimes we'll split them up and say, You use these ones this round and we'll switch next round. So all that is co-planned and the work is split up, which is very helpful.

However, the mentor formally assigned to her for this second year was teaching a special needs class and had never taught grade 4, thus limiting how much she could assist Tanya with program planning.

Tanya found planning for the older students challenging because "the program in grade 4 is much more driven by [government] curriculum expectations than it was in grade 1." But in general over the three years she became less confined by the formal curriculum because she

> learned how to read between the lines of the curriculum expectations. I've become better at saying, Okay, I know how that would look. When I first started, I'd read the expectation and only think of the expectation in one way – literally, that means they need to do this. Whereas I now see a variety of different ways of realizing the expectation.

One feature of Tanya's planning is her reluctance to use ability groups. She tends to form groups that are heterogeneous and changes them frequently. "I find that if I do ability groups my lower students get lost. And they're the ones I need not to be lost, they're the ones I need to be engaged." She now uses group work extensively, particularly in the literacy centers. Many teachers, especially beginning teachers, find group work problematic because of classroom management issues. In Tanya's philosophy of education, fostering a strong class community is essential if she is going to realize her vision of interactive learning. She spends an enormous amount of time in the first semester of each year building community, teaching social skills, playing non-competitive games during the Daily Physical Activity period, teaching students how to work in groups, developing a respectful culture, and establishing routines. As described below, her students truly work well together.

Tanya's Class in Action

Tanya's grade 3 classroom (in her third year) is a fairly large, bright room. The tables are arranged in groups and every inch of space is utilized. There are bins of books, crates of art supplies, baggies for the literacy centers, math manipulatives, photographs, books on display, samples of work, word walls reflecting the current units, motivational posters (that are changed regularly), a computer, and a teacher's desk tucked in the corner. The room is colorful and inviting.

One day when we observed Tanya's class, the complexity of her program was evident. The afternoon began with students presenting a Toy Expo. The science expectations for the term were force and movement, both fairly abstract concepts; however, the children had built toys embodying the concepts, using boxes, pipe cleaners, magnets, paper clips, elastics, springs, and so on. Each toy had to illustrate at least one force and one form of movement. The pupils wrote advertisements for their toys using the skills of persuasive writing they had learned in writing class. Another grade 3 class visited the Toy Expo and the scene was a true celebration of learning. The children were thrilled with their toys and could use scientific language to explain how they built them and how they worked.

The Toy Expo was followed by work at the literacy centers. The six centers were: persuasive writing (responding to the text, *Click, Clack, Moo, Cows That Type*); making words; listening (story on tape); reading comprehension (each student had an individually chosen book but answered generic questions); team reading; and spelling. There was a quiet hum in the room as the students worked in their centers for 30 minutes. The level of cooperation and time on-task was outstanding. The day ended with Tanya reading a chapter from *Jigsaw Joe* and leading pre-reading, during-reading, and post-reading discussion. Throughout the day, she moved among the children, giving words of encouragement, asking probing questions, and suggesting strategies. Her approach was caring yet firm.

Ongoing Professional Learning

In her third year, Tanya remarked that she will spend a lifetime learning how to teach. In every interview she described the many in-service workshops she attended, some focused on content (e.g., literacy) and others on instructional strategies. Both types deepened her vision for her program and strengthened her program planning abilities. By the end of the first semester of the first year, she had already attended three after-school workshops on literacy, had numerous meetings with the literacy consultant (all of which she arranged herself), and attended the monthly in-school PD sessions. In the second half of the first year, she went to a workshop "almost once a week."

As we have seen, Tanya's talents as a teacher emerged quite quickly. In her second year, the principal asked her to help co-plan a professional development session on instructional strategies. In her third year, she was invited to join several district-level professional development committees, including First Steps and the Schools Attuned Initiative. Participating in committees further increased her confidence and enhanced her own planning and implementation skills.

In conclusion, we can see that Tanya's undergraduate and graduate programs, with their strong academic content and extended practicum placements with able mentors, contributed to her solid formation as a teacher. By the end of her third year, her developed vision for literacy teaching, her deep understanding of child development, her extensive knowledge of balanced literacy, her familiarity with a broad range of curriculum resources, her repertoire of teaching strategies, and her reflective practice were evident in her very effective approach to program planning and teaching generally.

> **CASE STUDY ACTIVITY: In small groups, discuss the case study generally, then consider the following questions.**
>
> • What strikes you about Tanya's work?
> • What words would you use to describe her?
> • What do you think of her unwillingness to use ability groups?
> • How do you think that Tanya acquired such exceptional skills for program planning?
> • From this case study, can you identify Tanya's priorities for her literacy program?
> • Can you identify 10 decisions that Tanya made about her program?

Problems of Program Planning

Although all of the new teachers in our study soon recognized the need for program planning, they had great difficulty actually doing it. The challenges mentioned included:

1. **Preparing the formal "long-range plan" required by the school.** The new teachers had to submit this plan to their principal within the first few weeks, and most found the task daunting. Jody said that she

> needed to know how to make a long-range plan ... that was the first thing I had to hand in [to the principal]. And the only reason I sort of knew how to do it was because of a summer institute [I went to].

2. **Developing a working plan for the year.** Beyond this formal requirement, and much more importantly, the new teachers had difficulty
   developing a working plan for the year: feasible, balanced, integrated, sequenced, and complete with structures and routines. In
   June of her first year, Vera reported: "Long-range planning is still
   very challenging.... It's hard to know where I should be and where
   the students should be at this point in the year."

3. **Planning for the wide ability range in their class.** Jeannie said that
   "the biggest challenge is their starting off point ... some are already
   reading and some have no letter recognition at all." David observed:
   "I wasn't prepared for how hard it was to deal with mixed abilities;
   like it borders on the impossible some days." Candice, who had
   done a lot of unit planning in pre-service, commented:

> The language program I took last year was awesome ... [but] I
> know too much and it paralyzes me.... Knowing what a perfect
> program would look like and not being able to put it into
> action was frustrating: not being able to ... do all those things
> at the level at which all the different students need it.

Candice's experience is an example of the challenge of enactment
mentioned in the Introduction.

The decision-making role took many of the new teachers by surprise. To
what extent do you consider teachers to be decision-makers? What kinds
of decisions do you think would make you uncomfortable as a teacher?
Consider your teacher educators. In a class, think about the decisions they
made about the structure and content for that particular class.

Principles and Strategies of Program Planning

Although initially dismayed by the challenges, our study participants in
the end had much to say about how to do program planning. Based on
their comments and other sources, we outline below a number of principles and strategies in this area.

1. Recognize the Limitations of Formal "Long-Range Planning"

What needs to be understood is that a formal planning statement has
limited importance. It is usually just a listing of topics from the official
curriculum, sequenced over the year. It has some value as a document to

show to parents (often in abbreviated form) and to help us gain an overview of the official curriculum, but drafting it is a very small part of the
real task of program planning. Few teachers use it very much in their
teaching.

Moreover, the nature and significance of this requirement varies considerably from school to school. Principals differ in how comprehensive
they expect the plan to be. There are also variations in the help available
to develop the document. Maria reported that at her school small
groups of teachers do long-range planning "as a team, in all subjects,"
and Anna noted: "We have a school district resource disk where it's
click, copy, and paste.... It's got everything and every modification."
You need to find out as quickly as possible the expectations in your
school and utilize whatever help is given. Above all, you must distin-
guish between this largely formal requirement and the much more
important and demanding task of realistic, substantive planning for
learning in your classroom.

2. Identify Your Main Goals

Turning to the substance of program planning, a crucial step is to
identify your main goals for the year. Because time does not permit in-
depth coverage of all the topics in the curriculum (although you may
touch on all of them to some degree), you must have clear objectives to
which you give priority. This point was made by many of our new
teachers, especially in their second and third years. Toward the end of
her third year, teaching grade 4/5, Anita commented:

> We can't possibly cover all the content ... so we need to look at the
> big ideas or the main skills the kids require for success in a subject.
> So I often think about – and write down – what my goals are, what
> I'm trying to teach really.

Over the three years of the study, key goals for pupils mentioned by
the new teachers included:

- being able to read independently;
- selecting appropriate texts on their own;
- comprehending what they're reading;
- planning and generating ideas for writing;
- planning and structuring an information report;
- critical thinking;
- knowing how to approach research;
- enjoying interacting with peers;
- learning how to converse;

- being able to resolve conflicts;
- acquiring a sense of equity and inclusion;
- developing ideas about what is important in life.

While establishing a set of key goals, however, and even writing them down (as Anita does), you should not see them as fixed. Your interpretation of them will change as your students change and as you gain new insights into what is important. Also, you will keep adding to your list: over the years it will become quite long. At any given time, however, you will probably focus on a relatively small number of them, realizing that as you pursue one goal you will promote many others, as well. For example, as you teach the purpose of mathematics, you will also teach about the nature of numbers and how to apply mathematics.

ACTIVITY: During the Academic Program

In the core subjects, try to identify some of the key goals for each subject area. Keep your list fairly short so it is usable.

3. Establish Classroom Structures that Promote Learning

Many of our study participants stressed the importance of having class-room learning structures. Marisa said: "Structure helps, especially in the first year, because you know what to do and you don't feel you're picking things out of thin air.... I find that the more structure I have, the easier it is to plan." The learning structures mentioned by the new teachers included:

- learning centers;
- literature circles;
- guided reading;
- teacher reading to the whole class;
- regular independent silent reading;
- poem of the week;
- word study;
- writing scrapbook;
- book reports in varied formats;
- bell work;
- math challenge;
- extra activities when work completed early;
- Monday morning carpet sharing;
- culminating projects in varied formats.

4. Make Use of Textbooks and Programs

Even while being selective about goals, topics, and activities, we can still use texts and curriculum programs to a significant degree. Initially, many of the new teachers in our study felt they should develop their own units and lessons, or at least draw from a great many sources. They favored a "pick, choose, and create" approach to program planning. However, by their second or third year they began to see the limits of this approach and favored greater use of pre-set learning materials, though still with selection and modification. Among the advantages they noted in using textbooks and programs were the following.

a. **Saving time in lesson preparation and thus leaving room to be more creative in other ways.** As Maria commented:

> You might know all these strategies, but how do you teach them? Teachers don't want to waste all their time looking for books.... You want something that's easy to access, is available, and is related to the curriculum and to what the government says we need to do.

b. **Providing a basis for collaboration with colleagues using the same resources.** Vera tended to pick and choose in her first year, but in her second year she moved to a school where there was a great deal of collaboration, which in her view enabled her to "plan a lot more effectively." In New York City, Margaret and Natalie spoke in their first year about how much help they received from working with their literacy coach and grade team.

c. **Fostering professional growth.** Teachers can grow professionally as a result of using textbooks and programs and the accompanying resource guides (e.g., teacher manuals).

5. Be Flexible in Following Your Plan and Using Resources

The importance of flexibility in teaching was mentioned explicitly by all the participants in our study. In his first year, Paul reported: "I'm pretty flexible; often I'll have something I'm going to do and it doesn't really feel like the right thing, so at the very last minute I'll change it." Toward the end of his second year, David observed:

> Last year ... I seemed to be driven to get a lesson done within the set time; and then the next day there was a new lesson. And I think that was detrimental, because ... the students needed more time to

develop and reinforce the concepts.... So [this year] if the lesson didn't get done, it didn't get done; we'd do it the next day and just move forward with that.

One question that arises is *to what extent* individual teachers should deviate from the approach and materials chosen by their school or school district. As noted, there are advantages to having a common program in a school; and also teachers must protect themselves from being dismissed as mavericks (or literally dismissed). Some of the new teachers in our study said they kept quiet about their deviations. Several in their third year mentioned being taken to task by their colleagues for doing things differently, with remarks such as "You make us look bad" or "Why ever would you put so much work into it?" Among the New York City teachers, one said that she was expected to follow very closely a textbook that she did not regard as suitable, while another had much more flexibility and rarely used the set text.

As we weigh this issue, we should be aware that we often have more latitude than we think (although this varies from one country, state, and school district to another). Some of our participants commented that as long as their class was under control and the students were learning, the principal did not bother them. Tanya, while underscoring the courage it took, reported taking the position (in her first year): "No, I'm not going to do it. I understand I'm new, but I'm not doing that worksheet or teaching that way. I'm going to do it my own way." Obviously, we should figure out as quickly as possible how much divergence is feasible and appropriate in our particular context.

6. Adapt Your Program to Individual Students

Most of the new teachers in our study felt unprepared for the wide range of academic ability in their class, and some said this was their greatest challenge. This is an example of the complexity noted in the Introduction that is a challenge for some teachers. Wanda observed that even in a regular grade 1 class the academic spread "can be huge," requiring substantial program modification. Felicity, with a split grade 3/4, had enormous differences of literacy ability in her class:

I've got students who are reading at grade 1 level and others at grade 6. Some of my students are writing at grade 1 or 2 or not even that – some don't really even write, everything has to be scribed – while others are writing at grade 5. There are just so many different levels.

Although in our view the need is clear, individualizing instruction is only partly accepted in many schools and school systems. It is a matter on which a teacher may have to take a stand. Paul said at the end of his third year:

> The basic thing is that you have to start wherever the students are. And that is a problem because ... the curriculum assumes that they come to you with the previous year's material learned, but that's never the case with all or even most of the students. So ... for me the focus is still on what they need as opposed to what I'm supposed to cram in. And I'm becoming more and more a teacher who ... [is] going to do what the kids need ... and if someone wants to take me to task they can, and then I will explain why I'm doing it.

Paul had several students with severe behavioral problems in his class, and just by surviving he effectively won the right to insist on his approach. Teachers in other settings may have to be more careful in speaking about their individualization practices.

It is important to note that individualized instruction is *not* incompatible with whole-class learning methods. As we will discuss in Chapter 3, whole-class interaction is very important for community building, and furthermore students can help each other and learn from each other. The whole class is also a setting in which students can learn about each other's differences and acquire attitudes and skills of openness, inclusion, empathy, and conflict resolution.

While whole-class teaching is very important, many of the new teachers also advocated giving one-on-one attention to students. For example, Nina said: "[In the past] I focused too much on group work.... I should have spent more individual time with the children, because their needs are just so different." There are limits, of course, to how much individual attention teachers can give, so other strategies are needed. Wanda said that learning centers where students can work at their own pace and in their own way are beneficial to struggling learners in the lower grades. She also recommended getting the help of children's parents, having students work in pairs, and using a buddy system within the class.

7. Integrate Your Program

A vital means of establishing a strong program is to integrate it as much as possible – within, across, and beyond subjects (Allington, 2006; Meier, 1995; Wood, 1992). In our research, we saw an increase in program integration by the new teachers over their first three years. As they became more relaxed and got to know the content better, they found ways to link topics, units, and subjects more closely. There are several reasons for program integration.

a. **To save time.** Paul said that by "integrating math, science, and language into one unit you will cover a lot of things in less time."
b. **To increase student engagement.** Paul combines language arts with science because "it's really much more motivating for them, it's something they're interested in instead of just learning about words and sentences."
c. **To deepen understanding.** Most things in the real world do not fall under a single discipline (Wood, 1992). Integrated teaching enables students to understand subjects and specific phenomena more deeply.

8. Have Special Emphases in the First Few Weeks

Most new teachers find the early weeks of their first year very stressful. (This could partially be related to the apprenticeship of observation described in the Introduction: they do not really understand the nature of teaching since they have only observed it from the "outside.") This was certainly the experience of most of our study participants. They all survived and acquitted themselves well, but it was often quite painful and some felt they should have had more to offer their students at that time. While the principles of program planning outlined so far can certainly help, we need distinctive priorities, ideas, and strategies during the start-up period (Fountas & Pinnell, 2001; Jacklin, Griffiths, & Robinson, 2006). The special emphases required include:

a. **Establish a relatively structured program.** Because so much needs to be done and everything takes longer at the beginning, new teachers may have to follow a more structured approach than they would later in the year. David said that a beginning teacher should "find out what program the school board mandates and ... use it as a base, and then modify from there. Don't try to do it on your own because you'll just get overwhelmed." Liane recommended implementing "a very regular routine ... so it can be counted on: day after day you can expect that this is what needs to be done."
b. **Conduct preliminary pupil assessment.** During the early period we need to carry out relatively quick, informal assessment to get to know where the students are academically. Anita said a beginning teacher should "do some diagnostic assessing very early in the year ... to find out what the students' strengths are and what they need to work on." Jeannie stressed the need for "a September assessment ... trying to get them to write and see what they can do."

c. **Build the class culture and routines.** These matters should also be given special emphasis in the first few weeks, despite the pressure to begin to cover the curriculum quickly and get ready for the first report card. If the class community is well established, the time will be more than made up later in the year (Martin, 1992; Peterson, 1992). Toward the end of her third year, Sophia said:

> I spend a good two months at the beginning of the year work-ing on rapport.... And some people say I'm like a drill sergeant, but I'm now getting the best out of them because of it: I don't have to worry about management, all my attention is focused on the lesson and on them and what they're understanding.

d. **Go to others for help.** Many advocated seeking assistance from col-leagues during the early part of the year. Anita said a beginning teacher should "collaborate with other teachers as much as possible ... gather as many resources as possible and sit in on a few different teachers' programs to see how they are run, to get some ideas." Felicity also spoke of approaching others for help, although she noted it is not always easy: "When you're extremely overwhelmed [and] have no idea what you're doing and don't know what to ask for, that's a problem."

ACTIVITY: During Practice Teaching

During your placement in schools, take time to conceptualize the program planning role of the teacher and acquire some of the skills you will need as a teacher.

- Ask your cooperating teachers about the official curriculum. How much flexibility do they have? Do they follow it very closely? Find out how much leeway they have.
- Ask your cooperating teachers how they plan their lessons, their units, their year-long program. Try to get a window into their thinking. Ask them how they choose which topics to emphasize. If possible, plan a unit with them so you can witness the decisions they make.
- Look at the weekly timetable. Try to get a realistic picture of the time you *actually* have to teach. Factor into the timetable interruptions like community-building activities, assemblies, field trips, and special events.
- Find out the titles and publishers of the textbooks available for each subject and grade. Record this information and file it in your Resource Kit. Practice using the textbook by selecting activities, not trying to do everything. Become

aware of what kinds of activities you choose, why you choose them, and how they fit together.

- Become aware of the decisions you are making regarding program planning. Start to see yourself in the decision-making role.
- Get into the habit of sharing your materials and resources with other student teachers and teachers.
- Be prudent and thoughtful when accessing materials from the Internet. Judge the quality of the site. Bookmark quality sites. Look at the websites of professional organizations. For example, the International Reading Association site (www. reading.org/General/Default.aspx) is an excellent resource for materials.
- If possible, make photocopies of some of the resource materials your cooperating teachers have collected. Be judicious, do not photocopy everything. File and organize these materials immediately in your Resource Kit.
- Ask your cooperating teachers how they plan for the beginning of the school year. If possible, record some of their strategies and copy some of their materials. File them in your Resource Kit under "New School Year Activities."
- Look at the explanations of complexity and enactment in the Introduction. How do they apply to program planning?

Conclusion

Acquiring program planning concepts and skills should have very high priority in learning to be a teacher. From the outset, you should recognize that you cannot cover the whole curriculum in depth, and so must be selective and plan carefully. Components of program planning you need to master include:

- identifying your main teaching goals;
- being selective about topics and learning activities, in light of these goals;
- establishing structures in your classroom but also being flexible;
- individualizing your program;
- integrating your program;
- having distinctive priorities during the first few weeks of the year.

While effective programming is something you will continue to work on throughout your career, the aspects of planning reviewed in this chapter show many insights and skills you can learn during pre-service preparation and in your initial years of teaching.

Chapter 2

Pupil Assessment

Assessment is a normal part of the teaching/learning process, yet it can be a very challenging part of the process. All the new teachers in our study found assessment difficult and in many cases were overwhelmed by it. In addition to the sheer amount of time it took to assess pupils and write report cards, part of the challenge was knowing what to look for and how to assign a grade. These many aspects caused a fair bit of anxiety. Assessment of pupils is a very high priority in teaching and teacher education; however, there is considerable disagreement over precisely what form it should take and what role it should play.

PERSONAL ACTIVITY

As a student you have had many experiences of being assessed. Some were affirming, while others may have been devastating. Think about a time when you felt you were assessed *fairly*: this could have been in school, in a sports program, in a hobby group, or in another setting. Consider these questions.

- What information was gathered by the teacher, coach, or instructor?
- Did you know beforehand what you would be required to demonstrate?
- After the assessment, what information was given to you?
- How did the information help you improve?

Now think about a time when you felt you were assessed *unfairly*. Consider these questions.

- Why was it unfair?
- What impact did the experience have on you?

What have you learned from these two experiences that you can apply to your work as a teacher?

Reasons Why Pupil Assessment is Important

1. In order to do program planning, as discussed in the previous chapter, you have to assess what your students already know and can do, and what they are interested in.
2. As you implement your program, you need to find out which teaching methods are effective.
3. You must be able to report about your students' knowledge and skills to the students themselves, to parents, and to various bodies such as school districts, government departments, universities, and employers.

What is Pupil Assessment?

There are two main types of assessment. The first is *everyday teacher assessment*, which is a less formal type of assessment. Many teachers rely heavily on this less formal type of assessment yet it has to be comprehensive and systematic in order to give you the detailed knowledge you need of the students in your class, as a basis for supporting their learning. Cunningham and Allington, in *Classrooms That Work* (2007), say: "Assessment is *not* grading ... [and] *not* standardized test scores.... Assessment *is* collecting and analyzing data to make decisions about how children are performing and growing" (p. 160).

Similarly, Falk (2000) describes the role of such assessment as to "look at students and their work in an open-ended way to find out what they know, how they know it, and what their strengths and vulnerabilities are" (p. 41).

The second type of assessment is *standardized assessment*; it is standardized in that it assesses the same knowledge in the same way for all students. It measures a narrow band of knowledge and skills, and accordingly can only help with teaching to a limited degree. It is done mainly for school-wide, system-wide, and public purposes. Being standardized, it can be used to compare one student, class, school, school district, or government jurisdiction with another, again in limited ways.

ACTIVITY: During the Academic Program. Work in groups to fill in the following chart:

	Advantages	Disadvantages	When should it be used?	When should it be avoided?
Everyday teacher assessment (e.g., observation)				
Standardized assessment				

Make a glossary of assessment terms. Keep adding to it throughout your teacher education program.

Maria's Approach to Assessment: A Case Study

Now [in my third year of teaching] I have a better sense of how to do report cards. In your first year it's like, I think this kid does this; and when you go to the first parent–teacher interview, you hope the parent doesn't ask why you assigned that grade. Now I definitely have a better picture of what the students are capable of, because I know what to expect. You can't know that until you've been teaching for a year. It's almost not fair to ask first year teachers to give students a mark.

Background

Upon meeting Maria, one is initially struck by her commanding presence, yet she is warm and friendly. Maria completed a four-year Bachelor of Arts degree in Radio and TV Broadcasting. While in the program she did an internship at a national music video TV station, but realized she was more interested in the public relations aspect than on-air work. This led her to complete a year-long post-graduate program in public relations, and on graduating she secured a full-time position in public relations; but after 9/11 the firm downsized because their work in travel and tourism declined sharply.

Maria's mother had always encouraged her to consider teaching, so with "time on her hands" she began volunteering at the elementary school she had attended as a child. Realizing that teaching was a good match with her interests and skills, she enrolled in a one-year pre-service program specializing in Kindergarten to grade 6 with a focus on preparing teachers for urban schools. Over the three years since receiving her credential, Maria has been teaching grade 2 in the school she attended and where she volunteered. The neighborhood has changed dramatically since she was a student there; many of the families are struggling new immigrants living in low-rent/subsidized apartments and the school is classified as high needs.

Maria enjoyed her program in radio and TV broadcasting and believes it has helped her as a teacher because "quite obviously it's public speaking. You have to be comfortable with eye contact, talking to people, and hearing your voice. It was heavy on writing and grammar; we had a lot of English courses." She describes herself as someone who loves to read and write. Maria is also fairly positive about her pre-service program; in particular she enjoyed the literacy course, greatly admiring the instructor. She had two very successful practice teaching placements in grades 2 and 6, and her cooperating teacher from the grade 2 placement continues to be a mentor and friend. She feels that one of the limitations of teacher credential programs is that "you don't have any context, you're sitting there talking about ideal situations you haven't been in and they're not like that when you get into them. A lot of it gets washed away with reality." She would have liked very much to return to the school of education after her first year of teaching for "a summer program for people who have already taught for a year."

> I now have context. I'm not just saying, If I had a student like this …; rather I'm saying, Look, I have this kid who came to me on the second day of school…. Even though there was some context from the practicum, you had your mentor teacher doing all the organizing and all the day to day stuff.

Right from her first interview, Maria expressed strong interest in improving her assessment skills. In the first year she said: "I would love more PD on assessment. That was part of my [individual] annual plan. I want to improve on my writing program, especially, assessing writing." Maria is unusual because at an early stage in her career she has the "big picture" of assessment. She understands its connection to teaching: "It's reciprocal; we need the assessment to know what to teach." She feels that when you are planning a unit you must establish the goals for the unit and determine how it will be assessed. "It shouldn't be done at the last minute." She also feels that the students should be aware of these goals and criteria:

> [W]ith my kids, I put examples of journal stories on the overhead, a level 1, 2, 3, and 4. I'll put up a level 1 and we read it and talk about it. What level is this? Why? And the kids will say: Look at all the spelling mistakes; they repeat too much; not enough detail. So we start to create our own rubrics. Look at a level 2, a level 3, 4, and make your own rubric. Then I watch what happens when they go back and write their own journal story. It's fantastic, their writing is so much better because they know what you're looking for.

In her school, Maria is required to administer the DRA (developmental reading assessment); she finds it helpful for forming her guided reading groups, but sees its limitations.

I noticed a lot of kids were stuck at DRA Level 16, and I looked at that and said, You know what? I think it's the books. Look at the Level 16 book, it's about a mean man named Grumble and an elf. How much schema do my students have on elves? What do they know about that? There's no context. It's a difficult text for them.

Maria believes that she needs to work with children individually to truly determine what they have learned and ensure that no one "falls through the cracks"; for example, she uses miscue analysis, does conferencing with students individually, and designs a variety of work products for students to demonstrate what they have learned.

Learning Opportunities

In analyzing our interviews with Maria, we identified five key sources of her learning about assessment.

1. Pre-Service Program

Although Maria felt insufficient time was devoted to assessment in the pre-service program, she noted some aspects that were particularly helpful. In the literacy course, she was introduced to the mandated exemplars for assessing writing; then, using samples of student writing, she worked with a group "to compare the writing and decide if this is a Level 4 or Level 2." She said this stayed with her "because we did it." The assessment strategies used by the instructors were also a good model for her. "We used a lot of rubrics in the pre-service program, and I remember getting a project back and having the rubric all marked up. I realized the rubric told us exactly what they were looking for: you did it, and you pretty much got an A. And I realized I needed to do this with my own students."

2. In-School Support

The grade 2 teachers in Maria's school are very strong and work as a team, holding weekly planning meetings, sharing strategies and resources, and consulting with the in-school Literacy Coordinator. Although Maria works long hours – and in her first year felt as if she was "treading water, just trying to keep afloat" – some of the burden of planning has been reduced by working closely with the team, allowing her to develop assessment methods such as a modified miscue analysis form.

3. On-Going Professional Development

Over her first three years, Maria completed a reading specialist program, and the second course in the three-part program focused on assessment. Realizing she did not know how to interpret quantitative data, she suggested to the other members of her project group that they learn how to analyze DRA scores. All agreed, and she volunteered to share the DRA scores gathered on her in-coming students (the course was during the summer and the grade 1 teachers had tested each child). As a group, "we looked at all the scores, plotted them, and then looked for trends. We had different people doing different things. So I went into this year knowing where my kids were coming from, what they were capable of." She feels she now has a better understanding of ways to interpret data.

4. Induction Program

Maria was fortunate to be in a school district that offered a good induction program. She attended in-service sessions on various topics, including assessment. She and her mentor were provided release time to use as they wished and chose to spend time learning how to write report cards. Maria felt she wanted to see practice beyond her own school, so she observed an exemplary teacher in another school, paying special attention to her assessment strategies.

5. Leadership activities

As noted above, Maria participated in the district-sponsored induction program. In her third year, she volunteered to help with a Summer Institute for new teachers and became heavily involved in co-planning and co-teaching the sessions. "We spent three days with all the new grade 2 teachers and I showed them my year-long plan, my daily plans, and my weekly plans. We talked them through everything." Her support continued throughout the year "and we're having a Winter Institute [next year]. They're coming [to my class] and we're going to do guided reading with them. It's an extension of what we learned in the pre-service program." It supports her view "that [first] you have to teach, then you need to come back with the context." Through her work in the Summer Institute, Maria deepened her knowledge of all aspects of curriculum and assessment and gained an interest in assuming a leadership position in the future, possibly as a curriculum consultant.

Maria's Class in Action

Although Maria's grade 2 classroom is very old and in desperate need of refurbishing, she has made an effort to brighten the space by displaying student work, hanging charts from clotheslines, and creating a literacy centre. When the 20 students enter the room, Maria immediately calls them to the carpet to begin the math lesson. They are an extremely active group, but Maria has used a combination of well-established routines, humor, and community-building to focus their energy. For example, the class have been tracking the number of steps Maria takes each day by her wearing a pedometer and charting the number daily. They have fun predicting the number of steps she has already taken that day.

The class then turn their attention to a lesson on perimeter and area, with all the children eager to participate. The lesson is highly engaging, with students using magnetic blocks to compare the difference between the perimeter and area of various two-dimensional shapes Maria has drawn on charts. The students return to their seats to complete an excellent worksheet designed by Maria. All students are on-task and there is a quiet hum as they work. The students then attend a physical education class taught by a specialist teacher.

After recess, the students reconvene on the carpet for a class meeting because there has been an "incident" on the playground. Maria gently but firmly leads a discussion about community and the need for everyone to feel safe. Next, she shifts to a social studies lesson on festivals. Since it is close to Chinese New Year and many students in the class are East Asian, Maria has chosen to read a story about Imperial China. They discuss Chinese traditions, with plans to make lacey (red envelopes) for their families. They complete a worksheet on words related to Chinese New Year. Many students move seats to be with their friends, chatting as they work on their page. The day ends with them organizing their agendas and homework.

Final Thoughts

Maria is a fine young teacher working in a challenging urban school; her strength in the difficult area of assessment is an indication of her talent and progress. Over her first three years she has improved in all areas of teaching, gaining confidence as her students' learning increased: her class won a Reading Program Award for her school in 2007. She intends to continue her professional development, possibly enrolling in a Master of Education in the foreseeable future. Ideally, she would like to continue teaching grade 2 for at least another two years:

> Your first year is just survival, plain and simple. In the second year you're still trying to survive but getting a little better. In third year you start getting the gears in motion, you start bringing your ideas to the table. I can see myself next year bringing more to the program, and by year five having it come to fruition.

CASE STUDY ACTIVITY: In small groups, discuss the case study generally, then consider the following questions.

- What is the balance between Maria's use of everyday teacher assessment and standardized assessment?
- How did Maria link program planning with the information she gained from the various assessment methods used?
- Maria identified assessing writing as an area she needs to learn more about. What subjects or skills do you think will challenge you to assess? How can you learn more about assessing in this area(s)?

Problems of Pupil Assessment

Most new teachers find assessment difficult. Here we briefly outline the main challenges we have observed, discussing in the next section how they might be addressed.

1. Understanding the Nature and Role of Assessment

Teachers often begin with little understanding – and even deep *mis*understandings – about what assessment is and why it is important. This is due partly to their past experience of inadequate assessment methods in school and university, and partly to erroneous ideas about assessment prevalent in society.

2. Knowing How to Assess

In order to assess students in the comprehensive manner required, we need to use a wide variety of methods. Becoming familiar with these methods and skilled at using them requires a considerable amount of study and practice.

3. Being Able to Fit Assessment into the Busy Classroom Schedule

Our research on new teachers has indicated that, initially, many conduct very time-consuming kinds of assessment (e.g., comprehensive reading inventories, running records, miscue analysis) and as a result do not have time for other important kinds of assessment or other crucial teaching activities. Some become anxious because they think they *should* be doing assessment of certain types which they simply don't have time for.

4. Avoiding Doing Harm to Students

All types of assessment can go wrong if not used appropriately. Even *everyday teacher assessment* can be harmful if there is too much emphasis on "skills and drills" and rote learning of facts – e.g., word spelling, grammar rules, science formulas, historical dates – to the neglect of deep understanding and more important skills. With respect to *standardized assessment*, its common harmful effects have been well-documented in the research literature (e.g., Cunningham & Allington, 2007; Falk, 2000; Shepard, 2001; Shepard, Hammerness, Darling-Hammond, & Rust, 2005). These include:

- narrowing the goals of teaching to a sub-set, many of which are relatively trivial in nature;
- fostering in students an excessive preoccupation with fragmented information, test scores, and career advancement;
- stereotyping, ability-grouping, tracking, and grade-retention of pupils in ways that harm their self-image, increase their anxiety, reduce their learning, and disadvantage them academically and occupationally;
- simply wasting time through excessive teaching-to-the-test and coaching in test-taking skills, not to mention the time involved in the testing itself.

5. Challenges of marking and reporting

The new teachers we studied had a number of difficulties in marking and reporting:

a. **Too time-consuming.** Felicity: "I'm stuck with piles and piles of creative writing that I asked the kids to generate and I have no idea how to find time to mark it."

b. **Disparity between the current government assessment system and parents' understanding of grades.** Anita: "A lot of my kids get very discouraged if they're getting B's.... Parents are used to A's being good or being the best, but in the government curriculum B is at grade level and is actually very good."

c. **Parents not finding the report cards useful, intelligible.** Wanda:

> I think quite honestly that the report card for primary [Kindergarten to grade 3] does a disservice to the child and the parents: it doesn't really tell the parents how their child is doing.... We don't have the space or opportunity to really tell about the child.

d. **Discouraging students.** Anita said in her third year of teaching:

> [Assessment] is still one of the most difficult things I have to do;
> when I have a stack of papers to mark, I cringe at having to actually
> give a student a grade or a level. It's the least enjoyable part of my
> job.

Principles and Strategies of Pupil Assessment

We now present some of the principles and strategies of pupil assessment that we think can help meet the challenges in the area. In developing these ideas we have again drawn both on the literature in the field
and our longitudinal study of new teachers.

I. Connect Assessment to Teaching

The key step in developing a sound approach to assessment is to link it
closely to teaching. Problems arise when assessment is seen mainly as a
task performed for purposes other than teaching. Many of our study
participants' struggles with assessment were due to seeing it as separate
from teaching. When confronted with the enormous demands of teaching, especially in the first year, they wondered how they could find room
for assessment and why it was necessary to do so.

However, many soon saw that, far from being a time-consuming
"add-on," assessment properly done is an essential part of teaching; and
they overcame the problem of shortage of time by integrating assessment into their teaching activities. For example, Nancy reported:

> First of all, I have my students do something that's in my literacy
> program – a little assignment, a writing piece – to see where they
> are. And if I see they have a problem with tenses or use too much
> slang or whatever, I'll go and cover those things.

The degree of emphasis on connecting assessment to teaching grew
over time. For example, in March of her second year, Felicity said: "You
start to calm down a bit … in the second year, you start to be able to
observe the students better." She found she could incorporate much of
her assessment into her daily activities as a teacher:

> As you teach more, you start to make more visceral – for want of a
> better word – assessments. You know where your children are and
> what they're capable of…. [E]very day, you're doing little mini-
> assessments on the students and saying, "Well, their writing has
> improved" or "This is the area they're having difficulty with." So I

find I'm a lot more practical in how I'm using assessments; because it's "Oh this is what's happening, well let's address that," rather than pen-and-paper and marking assignments type assessment.

2. Limit the Emphasis on Standardized Assessment

The other side of the coin of linking classroom assessment to teaching is putting standardized assessment in perspective. It is crucial to view standardized tests as assessing only a sub-set of learnings, and so as being of limited significance for teaching (Darling-Hammond, Ancess, & Falk, 1995; Falk, 2000). Some special preparation in content and test-taking skills should be provided, because of what is at stake. But the main focus should be on fostering deep, important learning (Otero, 2006).

Initially, many of the new teachers in our study placed a lot of emphasis on formal reading assessment, especially Developmental Reading Assessment (DRA) which is a standardized form of assessment used in many schools. They were very concerned if they did not have time for this, and tended to give it priority over less-formal assessment. However, some saw the limits of this kind of assessment even in their first year. For example, Marisa in her first year said:

> I do the DRA … but also I try as much as possible to … just listen to the students reading, making sure they're reading something above their level.... [You need to] be on top of the students and keep pulling them aside for 5 minutes and listening to them read, because even that 5 minutes will give you so much information about what stage they're at and how they're doing.

Once again, we noticed progress over the years in the teachers' awareness of the limits – and in some cases the dangers – of standardized assessment. In her second year, Vera noted that she was now placing less emphasis on the DRA.

> One thing I [did differently this year] was … not just using DRA but using other things like their concept of print and how they see themselves as readers.... I'm still not totally sure how to use DRA effectively, but at least I see now that it's just one of many assessment tools you can use to see how to get at their learning.

By the third year, some of the teachers were quite vocal in their concerns about the government's large-scale literacy and math testing program organized by the Education Quality and Accountability Office (EQAO). David said:

Standardized testing – EQAO especially – drives everything we do.... And I'm thinking to myself, that represents what a kid did one day for three hours, it doesn't reflect who that child is. And just because a child scores a level 2, that doesn't mean they're not going to be Prime Minister of this country.... Our former Minister of Education was a high school drop-out. So to push these standards is to marginalize kids who can't perform on a paper-and-pencil test.

3. Use Many Kinds of Assessment

Once we see assessment as primarily to gain information for teaching, we realize it should ideally be as broad and individualized as teaching itself. Accordingly, many kinds of assessment are needed.

- Observation in the whole class.
- Observation in small-groups (guided reading groups, collaborative groups, centers, etc.).
- Observation in one-on-one settings.
- Self- and peer-assessment.
- Tests and assignments on specific topics.
- Open-ended assignments.
- Oral assessment.
- Written assessment.
- Collection and examination of rough work and polished work.

4. Develop a Feasible Program of Assessment

One of the main problems we saw in our study was that the new teachers tried (or hoped) to carry out types of assessment that were not really possible in the time available. This led to their feeling inadequate and frustrated; or, where they did do what they intended, they were left without time for other, more important, teaching activities and forms of assessment. It is essential that teachers develop an approach to assessment that is feasible. Part of the secret here is to integrate assessment into everyday teaching activities and the life of the classroom. Making notes on individual students has a place, but again it must be done in a feasible way. Do not embark on forms of documentation that are too time-consuming. Try to add just one new assessment method at a time and see how it goes. Recall from the Introduction the sheer complexity of teaching: this requires that you develop an assessment plan that is compatible with all the other things you must do as a teacher.

On the whole, the study participants became better at quick and informal (yet sufficiently comprehensive) kinds of assessment over the period of the study. In interviews toward the end of the third year, Paul said: "I'm not sure you have to make rubrics for everything and do the kinds of things that sound good in a workshop but that you really don't have time for." Anita noted:

> As they're working I go around and jot down little notes about how they're doing, or I ask them "Well, what are you doing today as a writer (or reader)?" and they tell me and I jot down where they are so that I can guide them better.... [Or] I make checklists for writing assignments – what's been taught and what's expected – and then check off what they've accomplished.

5. Individualize Assessment

Just as teaching must be individualized, as discussed in Chapter 1, so must assessment. For example, a student who is weak in formal writing may be strong in dealing with complex social situations, such as those found in the workplace or the community. Formal writing and other strongly "academic" skills should not be the only things that are assessed or reported. A more controversial aspect of individualized assessment is assigning grades to IEP (individual education plan/special needs) students and ELL (ESL) students because of their special needs.

> Talk to your cooperating teachers or school administrators about how to address the issue of special needs students.

6. Assess Authentically

If it is to be useful, assessment must be authentic, that is, "real" or "genuine." It must (a) *actually assess* what it sets out to assess, and (b) assess what is *important* from an educational and, ultimately, real-life point of view. The things we have been talking about so far – connecting assessment to teaching, de-emphasizing standardized tests, using many kinds of assessment, and individualizing assessment – all help ensure a focus on what we *actually* want to measure and teach rather than incomplete or superficial markers of learning.

Many of the new teachers in our study did not seem very aware of the need to connect schooling to the real world. They tended to focus on teaching government and school district "expectations" that are often standardized and removed from everyday life. Of course, there is a limit to the extent to which teachers – especially new teachers – can depart from officially mandated school learning. However, as discussed earlier, teachers often have more freedom than we think to decide which topics to emphasize and how much to relate them to the real world.

7. Marking and Reporting: Apply the Same Assessment Principles

Marking tests and assignments for reporting purposes is a somewhat distinctive activity. It is "summative," that is, *final* assessment aimed mainly at providing a grade, and is addressed in part to an outside audience (especially parents). However, in line with assessment in general, teachers should try to *connect marking and reporting to teaching* as much as possible. In this vein, Felicity commented:

> When I was younger in school, it was all about grammar and spelling. But from my teacher training program and being in the classroom, [I now think] we should focus on what we want to teach. So with the students' journal entries, I no longer cover them with red pen marks because what I'm looking for is that the students can express a concept or an idea or a feeling, and add detail into their writing.

Another general principle of assessment that applies to marking and reporting is to *use many measures*. The new teachers felt marks should be assigned on the basis of a variety of considerations, such as comprehension, writing skill, oral ability, work completion, and so on. For example, Marisa said:

> I'm trying not to rely too much on written responses as I find it doesn't always give me the best sense of what they know, because some of them – especially the boys – just write down as much as they need to finish and hand it in, not really showing you what they know. So writing isn't the best way to assess their reading, it's more their oral response, listening to their discussions and the questions they ask.

As with assessment in general, it is important to *mark and report authentically*. Some of the new teachers stressed the need to dig below the surface and capture what is really important for learning and for life beyond the school. Finally, in line with our earlier discussion, *marking and reporting activities should be feasible*. They should not take up so much time that teachers become exhausted or neglect other aspects of their role. Anita described how she saves time in gathering the information she needs for completing report cards:

I'm finding I'm much less stressed this year [year 2] doing report cards, because I'm circulating around my class all the time and always reading their writing and getting them to read to me and so on, so I have a better sense of where they're at, even if I haven't written it down. So I feel more confident that I'm giving them an appropriate mark this year than I was last year.

ACTIVITY: During Practice Teaching

- Ask your cooperating teachers what assessment measures (standardized tests) are required by the school district or government education department. If possible, look at a copy of a (previous) test. If the teachers are given a set of data on their students (e.g., test scores), look it over. If you have trouble interpreting the data, ask your cooperating teacher or school administrator to explain some of it to you.
- Choose three students in your class – low, medium, and high. Ask your cooperating teachers if you could see their report cards. As you read through them, what differences do you note?
- Choose one student you think is "interesting." Observe the student for a few days whenever you have a chance. What skills, talents, or abilities does the student have that you feel are not recognized by the formal school curriculum?
- If your practice teaching school is holding a parent–teacher night while you are in your placement, ask your cooperating teachers if you can attend one of the interviews. Note how the teachers interact with the parents, the information being conveyed, the level of discussion, and so on.
- If your students have a portfolio or a writing folder, flip through it. Look at the kind of material gathered and feedback they have received.
- Think about one of the units or strands that you teach during your placement. What are the big ideas for this unit? Ask yourself: How can I assess them?
- Practice doing everyday informal assessments. As you work with the students be mindful of the insights you are gaining into their learning. During recess, at lunchtime, or after school, jot down a few notes. As your placement continues, analyze the types of comments you are making: are they always focused on student (mis)behavior and particular skills like grammar and spelling? Do you include both positive and negative comments?

Conclusion

There are two main types of assessment: everyday classroom assessment and standardized assessment. The former is much more important than the latter, but unfortunately it often receives less attention in teacher education and writings on assessment. Classroom assessment enables you to find out about pupils' strengths, needs, and interests in the comprehensive way needed to support their learning. To do it successfully, you must understand the connection between assessment and teaching, and also have a large repertoire of authentic assessment methods that can feasibly be integrated into your teaching program and the life of the classroom. While acknowledging that there may be a place for standardized assessment, you should be aware of its narrow scope, the harm it can do, and the political forces at work in the design and imposition of testing programs. You should approach system requirements for standardized assessment in a way that minimizes the harm and leaves time for classroom assessment and key teaching activities.

ACTIVITY: For Your Resource Kit

- Collect and file samples of rubrics and assignments that you think are valuable.
- If the students do a very good culminating task for a unit either take photos of a few of them or photocopy them. File them under the relevant subjects.

Chapter 3

Classroom Organization and Community

A third vital aspect of the teaching/learning process is the *setting* in which teaching takes place: the physical layout, routines, social patterns, and atmosphere of the classroom. The setting does not just happen; it is deliberately fostered by the teacher. Every class, regardless of grade or subject, develops a particular culture. As you have probably experienced, some classroom cultures support learning and well-being while others can be toxic and detrimental.

PERSONAL ACTIVITY

Have you ever been part of a community that was very positive? The community could have been in a school, a sports group, a hobby club, or some other setting. What made it positive? How did it affect your learning/success? What can you take away from that experience that you could apply to your own teaching?

Why is Classroom Organization and Community Important?

1. The Classroom Setting is a Major Factor in Academic Learning

Students have difficulty learning if, for example, they:

- are constantly interrupted;
- are often unclear what to do next;
- feel unsafe or insecure;
- have little emotional connection with the teacher or their peers.

2. A Genuine Class Community Supports Social and Emotional Learning

Beyond academic learning, interpersonal experiences in the classroom can do much to help students grow socially and emotionally.

3. A Positive Classroom Environment is Important for Students' Well-Being

Apart from learning, the school classroom is where young people spend much of their time for up to 14 years of their life; it is a large part of their universe. The nature of their experience there is crucial to their well-being. As Wanda, one of the new teachers, said:

> [F]or me, as a grade 1 teacher, success is having a student or a student's parents tell me that they want to be at school by 7:30 because they want to be the first one in the class. That tells me that hopefully I'm doing something right in terms of creating a nurturing and safe environment and encouraging them to want to learn and love books and just enjoy school.

4. A Positive Classroom Setting is Also Essential for the Well-Being of the Teacher

Teachers must be able to survive, remain strong, and enjoy what they do – despite the rigors of teaching – and this is more feasible if they are in a friendly and well-functioning classroom. As Felicity commented at the end of her third year of teaching:

> Now that I've done it a few times, I'm looking for ways to make teaching easier without compromising the level of interest and activity in the classroom.... I'm also looking to enjoy myself more in the classroom. So, I have to figure out how I can do that. How can I make it so it's less stressful for me, and less exhausting, but the children are still getting quality teaching? And I think, really, that breaks down into organization and classroom management, those two. If you can get those two going, then you can really save yourself a lot of stress.

What is Classroom Organization and Community?

Classroom organization includes much more than just rules; it includes the whole class culture and community, which is integrally linked to learning. The importance of the classroom setting is emphasized in the educational literature. Writers such as Martin (1992), Noddings (2005), and Peterson (1992) stress the need for affection, caring, and community in the classroom. Zemelman, Daniels, and Hyde (1998) state that "the socioemotional development of the classroom community" should be a major concern of the teacher (p. 192).

1. Rules, routines, class values, student groupings, classroom management, class community, and the teacher–student relationship are all interconnected elements.
2. The class community includes social and emotional elements as well as academic ones.
3. Student well-being is an essential ingredient in classroom life.

Anita's Approach to Classroom Organization and Community: A Case Study

Part of building community is me treating students with respect, talking to them respectfully, and not being condescending. When the students feel they are valued, respected, and listened to, then they feel safe and secure. They feel they can do their best work and they pass that respect on to others and to the teacher.

Background

Anita, a gentle, thoughtful teacher in her late twenties, completed a one-year post-baccalaureate pre-service program at OISE/UT with a specialization in teaching history (or social studies), giving her the credential to teach grades 4 through 10. In her initial three years of teaching, she worked in two markedly different schools, teaching a grade 5 class in literacy and math the first year and a combined grade 4/5 class the next two years with responsibility for most curriculum subjects. In the first year, she was not able to secure a permanent position until October, when she was hired to teach mornings only a newly formed grade 5 class with students drawn from the other grade 5 classes in the school. This urban school had a high proportion of minority students, mainly of Middle Eastern, South Asian, and South-East Asian heritage, most from a low socio-economic background. Her first year of teaching was extremely challenging because her students understandably resented being uprooted from their original classes in mid-semester, and many were performing well below grade level; but, in spite of the situation, she successfully built community. She felt supported by the principal and other teachers, and worked much longer hours than her half-time appointment required.

Anita's undergraduate degree included a double major in psychology and linguistics, which she felt was a useful background for teaching. Her pre-service program was cohort-based and framed by a social constructivist philosophy, with the principles of inquiry, integration, and community shaping the curriculum and the entire experience. The faculty in the program spent substantial time building community through a range of activities: a two-day retreat at the beginning of the year, cohort socials for students and faculty throughout the year, explicit discussion of community and learning, and modeling of collaborative learning techniques such as literature circles. She noted that the program had a strong influence on her goals and practices as a teacher:

> I came away from pre-service with this feeling that I wanted to build a positive community in my class, and that has been an explicit goal on my part. I didn't really have that as a goal going into the program, so I think it affected me that way ... drawing my attention to how important community is.

The importance of community and the need for effective classroom management strategies were reinforced in Anita's practice teaching placements. One of her mentor teachers excelled in building community:

> Marg was very into treating students with respect and making sure everyone felt comfortable. I learned that you have to have a strong community before any sort of deep learning can take place.... How Marg spoke to the students and how she dealt with the students showed that she had a great deal of respect for the students and they could tell that. She had an amazing manner about her, very approachable, very respectful.

Anita felt she learned a great deal about classroom management from her instructors in the academic program, many of whom were experienced teachers; they spent considerable time addressing relevant goals and strategies. Also she participated in Tribes training (Gibbs, 2000) during the program, which helped her learn additional principles and strategies.

Description of Practice

We found Anita to be exceptionally able in classroom management and community building. Her classroom has a calm atmosphere; students work well together; there is a spirit of support and collaboration; routines are firmly established; student misbehavior is dealt with swiftly but

in a positive way. Anita knows her students well; students are responsible for maintaining a supportive culture; very difficult students are
repeatedly given inviting messages to join the community; and humor is
used to diffuse tense situations and create a unique class culture. Anita
believes it is "the teacher's responsibility to keep the kids engaged. I
don't think we should put the onus on the kids.... It's our job to facilitate their engagement, how they're interacting with each other and
approaching their work."

Anita's skills evolved over the three years. She came to see more
clearly that community does not just "happen"; she purposefully
engages in community-building activities, employing many of the strategies that were used in her pre-service cohort. At the heart of her philosophy is the belief that it is essential to know her students as individuals,
becoming aware of topics that interest them or challenges in their home
situation. We can see the influence on her of the social constructivist
philosophy of her teacher education program. She recalled learning in
the program

> the theory of how to facilitate kids talking about books and figuring
> out the parts they enjoyed and making the experience enjoyable for
> them.... If it doesn't have meaning for them, they're not going to be
> engaged and excited by reading and writing.

Anita recognizes that community-building is not restricted to formal
Tribes activities or other special techniques; it also has to be part of her
regular academic program. For example, she employs a range of class
groupings: whole class, self-selected groups, ability groups, teacher-
selected groups, randomly created groups, and individual work.
Throughout the day, students have many opportunities to interact with
each other. She reconstitutes the groups regularly to prevent ability
grouping from harming student self-esteem.

Group work can be challenging for beginning teachers. Around the
middle of her first year of teaching, Anita formed guided-reading
groups, but she found the management of them somewhat problematic.
The principal, a very effective curriculum leader, offered suggestions for
program planning and also arranged for Anita to observe experienced
teachers managing group work. Through these observation sessions
Anita came to realize that changes in her practices were needed,
although she was reassured to find that classroom management is an
on-going concern for all teachers. She became stronger in establishing
routines and effective group activities, and making her literacy program
more engaging for her students.

By the third year, Anita's skills in classroom management were exemplary. Of special note is the way she makes expectations for student

work and behavior transparent, in part by involving students in setting expectations. The following is an example she gave of how she does this:

> In first term, the students learned many writing skills, and for their final project they needed to use all these skills. Before they wrote the project I said, "Based on what we've been learning, what do you think I'm going to assess you on?" They gave me a list of all the things that we had been doing in class. I added one or two points and then I said, "Okay, this is a checklist of how I'm going to mark you." We also talked about what levels 1, 2, 3, and 4 [on the rubric] might include. I find creating rubrics with the kids helps a lot.

Anita's Class in Action

At the end of her second year, Anita was declared "surplus" at her original school, but luckily she secured a position in a neighboring school, also in the core of the city but in an area undergoing gentrification. The students come from both affluent and less-well-off families. The staff are welcoming, helpful, and cohesive, with a principal who has a very democratic approach to decision-making. Anita sees the staff as a community and feels there is a collective sense of responsibility for the children's learning and well-being.

Anita's classroom is bright and cheerful, with student work in art and core subjects on display. Motivational posters line the walls and charts with helpful hints for working with others are hung across the room. On a day when we visited her, students eagerly entered the classroom and were warmly greeted by Anita who asked specific questions or made encouraging comments, clearly revealing her knowledge of each child. It is a combined grade 4/5 class yet the students mingle easily with each other. The day began with an imaginative word-study exercise where each student gave a presentation on 10 words they had selected during their independent reading that they found interesting or believed could help them with their writing. As the students shared their words, the rest of the class listened closely, and all were comfortable asking or responding to questions. Some students presented on quite advanced vocabulary while others had chosen simpler words, yet there was general support for all. When one student made an inappropriate comment, Anita reminded him about the type of talk allowed in their community. It was a firm but not aggressive response.

The students then moved to the bank of computers in the library to work on their social studies projects. They were using the computer program Smart Ideas to generate a web of ideas on a social studies topic, followed by a final report. Although these were individual projects – on citizenship and the rights and responsibilities of governments – the children helped each other. For example, one student was not sure where to put agriculture on her web because, as she said, "it is not really a natural resource." As students made suggestions, it was apparent they had learned skills and attitudes for giving feedback and assisting each other. All were on-task, but they also conversed easily about personal interests (*Are you going to try out for the swim team?*) and the social studies project (*How many ideas do you have in your web?*).

During recess, Anita worked with students in the folk dancing club she organized. There was a strong sense of camaraderie among the students and between her and the students as they practiced their dances. After recess, Anita gave a presentation to the whole class on the mathematics of making change. She then divided them into heterogeneous groups she had pre-selected to work on making change for various "purchases" from the class store. She made clear beforehand the expectations, for example that each student must have a turn and group members are responsible for helping each other. When the class became too noisy, she used a rain stick to get their attention. At the end of the group work, Anita had the whole class reconvene to debrief on the process of the group work and their learning, which they did honestly, respectfully, and with humor. They ended the class with thumbs up, thumbs down, or thumbs in the middle to assess the effectiveness of their group.

Final Thoughts

Anita's pre-service program and the two schools where she taught advocated class community, but this only partially explains her success in fostering a dynamic learning community. She is guided by a vision for her class that extends far beyond completing the mandated curriculum expectations. She truly sees teaching as a relational act between herself and the students, and between herself and the other teachers, and she believes in students supporting each other's learning and well-being. She also understands the links between program planning and community building: her program supports the growth of community and the strong community allows her to offer an engaging program. Her sunny disposition, her warm manner, her clear understanding of the role of the teacher, her thoughtfulness in all her interactions, her willingness to learn from others, her high expectations for the pupils, her effective classroom management strategies, her efforts to involve parents in their children's schooling, her engaging curriculum, her wisdom about life, and her commitment to her students are all elements that contribute to her class becoming a community.

CASE STUDY ACTIVITY: In small groups, discuss the case study generally, then consider the following questions.

- What are the links between Anita's strong class community and her students' learning?
- What does respect "look like" in Anita's class?
- Anita is *friendly* to her students but not *their friend* in the ordinary sense. What are the differences?
- In what ways does Anita's classroom compare to the practice teaching classrooms where you have worked or ones where you have volunteered?

Problems of Classroom Organization and Community

Establishing effective structures and a positive community in the classroom is beset by many challenges. For student teachers, the long apprenticeship of observation described in the Introduction is particularly relevant because it may have given you an unsound approach to the classroom. Often, as student teachers, you want to be friends with your pupils, which can make classroom management difficult because the pupils get confused about the teacher's role. Classroom management often consumes a great deal of emotional energy, and when pupils rebuff your efforts and continue to misbehave, you are taken by surprise. Probably this type of misbehavior occurred when you were pupils but you were unaware of the struggles your teachers faced.

1. Disruptive Student Behavior

This was a problem mentioned by all the participants in our study. While they were usually able to keep order in their classroom – things rarely got out of hand – the behavior problems meant that a lot of time was wasted, some learning activities were simply not feasible, and the stress level rose for teacher and students alike. Nina (teaching grade 2) commented:

> [O]ne of the biggest issues I have in my class is behavior.... I have one student who's on Ritalin, and when he doesn't take his medication it changes everything. I've got another student who I think is ADHD, but I'm still [in March] trying to have him diagnosed. He simply cannot sit in his seat. I have another child who is ELL and because of his language frustrations and his personality, he's throwing scissors across the room. Behaviorally it has just been a

big challenge. So in my literacy program it's very difficult. For example, guided reading, in theory I love ... [but] in my class it doesn't work.

2. Difficulties of Small-Group Work

Many of the new teachers in our study said they did not know how to implement small-group learning in the classroom: how to make it effective and how to keep students on-task.

3. Justifying Collaboration and Community

A general problem with collaborative, community-oriented classrooms is that, even when teachers and students enjoy them, they often do not see them as "real school." Often the concept of community is dismissed as too "flaky" to be an essential part of schooling. This places a burden on teachers to explain – and *show* – why this approach is indeed valuable. In some cases, the new teachers in our study did not seem fully convinced of it themselves.

ACTIVITY: During the Academic Program

As a teacher, sometimes less is more. The fewer rules you have the easier it is to maintain a well-run classroom. Work in groups on the following activity. Brainstorm a list of rules (e.g., no swearing in the classroom) and routines (e.g., tidying up the classroom before dismissal) that should be established at the start of the school year. Discuss the importance of the items on each list. To what extent do you need rules and routines? (Do not be surprised if there are very different viewpoints in your group.) Then you should all rank the three rules and routines you believe should be given top priority. Compare your rankings with each other. Every teacher has a different set of priorities. By identifying what is important to you, you will know what to focus on as a teacher at the beginning of the school year.

ACTIVITY: For Your Resource Kit

Ask your cooperating teachers about letters of welcome they send home to students' families at the start of the school year. Also ask about community-building activities they do with their students at the start of the year. File this information in your Resource Kit under School Start-Up Activities.

Principles and Strategies of Classroom Organization and Community

The new teachers in our study made considerable progress over the three years in the complex areas of group work, classroom management, classroom organization, and class community. Recall the challenge of enactment from the Introduction to this book on pages 4–5. Enacting or developing the type of classroom you have in mind is often quite difficult. Think about the challenge of enactment when your class is not matching the idealized version you have pictured. Here we present some principles and strategies in this area, drawing on our study participants' views and practices along with other sources.

1. Build Community in the Classroom

Successful small-group and whole-class learning requires a strong class community: community is not a frill. Peterson (1992) states: "When community exists, learning is strengthened – everyone is smarter, more ambitious, and productive" (p. 2). According to Dewey (1938), "education is essentially a social process" (p. 58).

Many of the new teachers in our study supported a social emphasis, outlining some of the strategies they use to foster community. For example, Wanda said:

> I try to incorporate some of the Tribes approach: the concept of building community, building a team, and understanding that we have to respect one another and have kindness and trust in the classroom. Together we sit down and look at the type of classroom rules we want, what we expect of one another, and the importance of listening attentively to each other. And that was a theme throughout the year.... They got tired of hearing me say that the more friends you have the better off you are.

Nina, in her third year, described how she focuses on

> four tenets: cooperation, kindness, honesty, and choices ... and I work with those words and have them understand them deeply. And I make it clear there is no tolerance for laughing at each other, no tolerance for bullying.... And if there's a problem at recess, I say "I can't believe that someone in my class would do that."... So I think that within my classroom, most of the children feel safe and that they can be themselves, and we work as a team for the most part.

2. Take a Broad Approach to Classroom Management

Good classroom management is a crucial aspect of classroom life, necessary both for learning and student and teacher well-being. But trying to manage a class through rules alone does not work. Many teachers today are experimenting with "zero-tolerance" classroom management, instituting a detailed rule system and stopping the class almost every time a rule is broken. However, on the whole this approach is not effective. Students lose interest when learning activities are constantly interrupted and they focus instead on trying to out-maneuver the teacher. Also, animosity builds between teacher and students.

Classroom management is inseparable from everything else we discuss in this book and chapter. It involves working on many fronts at once (Evertson, Emmer, & Worsham, 2006; LePage, Darling-Hammond, & Akar, 2005) which is all part of the complexity of teaching described in the Introduction. For example, it requires:

- well-chosen topics of study that engage students, meet their individual learning needs, and as far as possible relate to their lives;
- a variety of learning activities;
- ways of doing things in the classroom, so students know what is expected;
- firmness on the part of the teacher: quick action where needed;
- kindness on the part of the teacher: acting with humor, care, and interest in the students as human beings;
- a strong class community that students enjoy and within which they see themselves as valued members who have responsibility for other members – including the teacher.

The new teachers in our study had many useful ideas about classroom management. Felicity observed that if you "keep it interesting ... that helps with your classroom management." Vera talked about the need to balance firmness with friendliness in relating to students, maintaining "a positive climate while keeping structure." Paul described how he relies on class dynamics to help with classroom management:

There are students who are really good at class "citizenship": belonging to the community, getting along, finding solutions to problems.... I've seen a few students really shine: they know what to say to people and how to get the whole class calmed down or listening or doing what they're supposed to.

3. Get to Know Your Students as Individuals

A good relationship between teacher and students is essential for an effective and positive classroom. The teacher has to take the lead in advocating community, setting up community structures, and modeling attitudes and relationships essential to community-oriented education. While classroom democracy is important, the teacher is a key figure in the classroom, charged with establishing the agenda, making final decisions about what is acceptable, and setting the tone. As Felicity said:

> With the atmosphere in your classroom, you really have to start from the top. You need to be positive and create that atmosphere in yourself, and that is what your classroom will be like.... You have to decide, what kind of classroom do I want to be in, and would I like to be in as a student?

Jody, who in year 3 was working with special needs students, said:

> I'm guided by the thought: imagine going to a place where you fail every day. And these kids do.... So I always try to be supportive. I push them as much as I can to get them to learn, but I do it in a really positive way.

Paul commented:

> [W]hen you tell a student, "You need to stop doing that, you need to do this, you need to learn that, you need to do your homework," if they really have no relationship with you – or the relationship is negative – they're not going to follow what you say.

Along the same lines, Nina observed: "I need to use respectful language and treat each child with respect. Because if they see me more in a kind of master–slave relationship, how can I expect them to treat the other students – and me – with respect?"

4. Balance Small-Group, Individual, and Whole-Class Activities

Individual work is crucial for a number of reasons.

- Students' abilities, interests, needs, and styles vary so much that they must often be allowed to work on their own (even when *sitting* in groups).

- Students must move beyond being passive recipients of knowledge and see learning as something *they* do for their own reasons, not just something done *to* them.
- Students need *practice* in taking charge of their own learning, assessing their own strengths and weaknesses, and being proactive in building their knowledge and skills.

Whole-class activities are also very important in the classroom (Kohn, 1999; Zemelman et al., 1998). Among the new teachers in our study, Paul in his second year spoke of the need for whole-class activities. "Because of all the [behavior] problems [this year], I've been doing more on just getting the whole class on the same page and working together." Whole-class activities are necessary because:

- they provide variety, and are often more engaging than individual and small-group work;
- students like to get to know others in their class and hear what they have to say;
- students like to feel they belong to the whole-class community;
- whole-class work can often be easier for the teacher to manage and a more efficient method of teaching certain topics;
- whole-class activities play a crucial role in community building (Peterson, 1992).

5. Develop Effective Approaches to Group Work (Small-Group or Whole-Class)

Despite the challenges, small-group work can often be very valuable in the classroom. If well-planned and implemented, it can enhance the effectiveness and enjoyment of learning (Barone & Morrow, 2003; Kohn, 1999; Zemelman et al., 1998). The challenges, then, do not mean that small-group work should be avoided, but that you should be *selective* in using it (Allington, 2006; Bainbridge & Malicky, 2004; Zemelman et al., 1998). You should not see it as *the* main teaching approach. In December of her first year, Tanya, who is a very able teacher, said:

> I haven't been able to set up literacy centers and guided reading groups.... Some teachers would start these in September, but I wasn't experienced enough to know how to set up these routines without the students having some independent skills.

If you are to employ group work – and convince your students and others of its value – you must figure out how to do it well. Cossey and Tucher (2005) raise the question, "What will make a collaborative effort worth your while?" and go on to suggest some key principles (pp. 116–117):

- ask yourself if the project ... is sufficiently complex and interesting;
- consider whether each individual [in the group] has something in particular to do;
- [ask whether group members] hold a diversity of perspectives;
- ask ... whether a collaborative effort is worth your time [on this occasion].

Other principles could be added, such as:

- explain to students the purposes of group work;
- train students over time in particular group methods;
- provide clear instructions for an activity, often in writing;
- choose a group size that matches the task and age level (usually, the younger the students, the smaller the group);
- vary the group methods used (both to heighten interest and to enable more students to get to know each other).

> The central questions underlying many of these principles is: *What will the students learn from this group activity, and why will they learn it better through group work rather than other methods?* When you are teaching be mindful of the grouping – large or small group – and ask how this type of group will support learning.

Many specific collaborative methods are described in the literature. Examples include:

- peer tutoring, assessing, and editing;
- working in twos and threes;
- think, pair, share (often a three-stage process from the individual to the whole class);
- guided learning (where a small group works with the teacher);
- literature circles (like book clubs);
- learning centers (different activities in different locations around the room);
- group projects (where the group develops a product together);
- "jigsaw" activities (where discussion preparation tasks are divided among group members);
- whole-class discussion;

- whole-class debates;
- simply going around the room (with the opportunity to "pass").

Many of these activities work well in combination: for example, jigsaw followed by reporting back to the whole class.

6. Limit the Use of Ability Grouping

When teachers do employ small groups, on what basis should they be formed? We believe that using ability as the criterion is questionable (Atwell, 1998; Peterson & Hittie, 2003). According to Zemelman et al. (1998): "One of the signal contributions of educational research has been the explicit rejection of tracking and the affirmation of hetero-geneous grouping" (p. 258). A common argument for ability grouping is that less-able students feel more comfortable in a separate group, but in fact placing students in a lower group usually makes them feel *less* comfortable overall.

Moreover, research suggests that ability grouping is not sound even from an academic point of view (Atwell, 1998; Cunningham & Alling-ton, 2007). More-able students usually do no better academically when grouped together (Bainbridge & Malicky, 2004), and less-able students do significantly worse because expectations (both theirs and their teach-ers') are lowered and they have less exposure to "more skilled perform-ances" (Darling-Hammond, 1997, p. 131).

Many of the new teachers in our study said they largely avoided ability grouping. For example, Paul said: "I like to do things in groups [but] I think it's important to switch the groups, not to have the same groups all year, and give the students a bit of say in the groups."

7. Emphasize Inclusion and Equity

All the elements of a positive classroom setting discussed so far – pro-ductive small-group and whole-class work, a vibrant class community, effective classroom management, and a close teacher–student relation-ship – are in turn dependent on respecting students' diverse personalities and backgrounds. Without such respect, students will not be inclined to collaborate with one another, participate in the class community, or develop a fruitful relationship with their teacher. Respect for students has many aspects, but a key one is respecting racial, ethnic, gender, and other differences, and ensuring that all students feel accepted in the class. How to foster such respect and acceptance will be discussed at some length in Chapter 4.

ACTIVITY: During Practice Teaching

- As you walk through the main entrance to the school, look around – does the entrance welcome or discourage visitors? What posters and information are on the walls? What "messages" do these send to students, teachers, and visitors?
- During your first week in your placement, record every routine and rule your cooperating teacher has established. Try to follow them closely when you are teaching these students.
- How would you describe the atmosphere in your practice teaching class? Why has this culture developed? To what extent does it support and/or hinder student learning?
- Some students are very congenial while others require us to make more of an effort. Choose one student whose behavior is somewhat problematic. Spend time getting to know that student (e.g., favorite TV shows, sports, foods). What parts of school does the student actually enjoy? Try to find out why the student acts inappropriately. What could be done (academically and socially) to help the student?
- Ask your cooperating teachers how their classroom management practices have evolved over the years.
- Look at the explanations of complexity and enactment in the Introduction to this book. How do they apply to classroom organization and community building?
- At the end of the day, ask yourself if you and your students laughed at least once that day.
- Be gentle with yourself. Think about ways in which you are making a difference in the lives of your students.

Conclusion

While program planning and everyday assessment are crucial for pupil learning, equally important is the setting in which the learning occurs. Key aspects of the classroom setting are a strong class community, getting to know your students as individuals, and full inclusion of students of various backgrounds. These elements in turn will assist with the much-discussed problem of classroom management, as students feel they are respected and accepted within the class community.

Chapter 4

Inclusive Education

As you work in schools you will notice that many are highly heterogeneous, the students having a range of backgrounds and abilities.
Related to this diversity, another very high priority in teaching is "inclusive education." We use this term broadly to refer not only to inclusion
of "special education" students in the classroom, but also addressing
appropriately other differences, such as those of gender, race, ethnicity,
mother tongue, and socioeconomic status.

PERSONAL ACTIVITY

Think about the elementary, middle, and high schools you
attended. Would you describe the student population as fairly
homogeneous or heterogeneous? To what extent did you get to
know students who had backgrounds different from your own?
Would you like to teach in the kinds of schools where you were
a student? The values held by your family most likely influenced
you a great deal. What values around diversity and inclusion
were emphasized in your family? How did these influence you as
a student? How will they influence you as a teacher?

Why is Inclusive Education Important?

1. Students need to feel safe, accepted, and respected if they are to be
   able to concentrate, take risks, and participate in class learning
   activities.
2. Beyond academic considerations, feeling respected and accepted is
   also crucial for social participation, social learning, and general
   well-being.
3. Students need to understand the phenomenon of prejudice and discrimination, and acquire inclusive outlooks, attitudes, and behavior
   patterns.

4. Equal treatment of students is supported by general ethical and political arguments, and is also an underlying assumption of progressive, constructivist education.

What is Inclusive Education?

In earlier decades, the term "inclusive education" usually referred to the practice of placing "special education" students – that is, students with "disabilities" – in mainstream classrooms. However, the broader usage we follow here is now becoming more common. Ainscow, Booth, and Dyson (2006) say that, in keeping with a trend emerging "internationally," the aim of inclusion in education is "to reduce exclusion and discriminatory attitudes, including those in relation to age, social class, ethnicity, religion, gender and attainment" (p. 2). Similarly, Verma, Bagley, and Jha (2007) observe that:

> [A] plethora of critical literature has emerged recently, re-examining the concept of inclusive education from an educational reform perspective. Schools in this critical perspective should respond and adapt to the needs of *all* children, regardless of gender, physical, cognitive and sensory needs, ethnicity and religious and cultural background.
>
> (pp. 33–34)

Even with agreement on this broad definition, however, at least three "dilemmas" remain about how inclusive education should be implemented. We can:

1. address inclusion mainly through separate lessons and units, *or* largely "infuse" it into the academic program and the life of the classroom.
2. focus mainly on understanding and respecting the differences between people of various races, ethnicities, classes, and so on, *or* stress commonalities as well as differences.
3. have a constructivist approach to fostering an inclusive outlook, allowing it to emerge in students as they respond to information, discussion, and classroom experiences, *or* take a relatively authoritarian, "top-down" approach to inclusion.

The view we wish to recommend is that inclusive education should largely be infused into the program and life of the classroom; focus on commonalities as well as differences; and be constructivist rather than top-down in nature.

ACTIVITY: During the Academic Program

Discuss in small groups what position you would take on each of the three dilemmas above. Would you adopt one or other of the alternatives or something in between?

Paul's Approach to Inclusive Education: A Case Study

> I have kids who have seen people getting shot, they've seen people being stabbed, they've seen lots of drug dealing and prostitution with their own eyes, regularly. So these kids have a different point of view.

Background

Paul came to teaching after spending eight years as an architect. Having immigrated from Korea with his family at an early age, he had been involved in his youth in the local Korean community where his father was a minister. He taught both Sunday school and violin to members of his church; although very musical, he did not consider pursuing a degree or career in music. His first three years of teaching after completing his credential program were in an extremely high-needs urban school where all the children live in subsidized or low-rent apartments. As the opening quote indicates, many of his students do not have "traditional" life experiences.

Paul's school, with approximately 550 children, aims to build community and reach out to the community. Many students belong to visible minority groups, many are English Language Learners (ELL), and a high proportion are designated as special needs. Such diversity is attractive to Paul, who has a strong commitment to public schooling. In a year 3 interview, he said:

> For me, public education is very important.... I think segregating people at too young an age in a culture is just not good. Even if it's harder to have them together, and even if they do not excel as much academically, the benefits far outweigh the costs.... I don't think being powerful and rich is as important as culture. I would actually rather live in a poorer country where people get along.... I want people to have a good quality of life and help each other have a good quality of life, even if it means they drive a Honda rather than a BMW.

For the first two years, Paul taught grade 5, and in his third year he taught a small class of boys who were "learning disabled," many of them with "behavioral" difficulties. As a former ELL student himself, he feels he can relate to some of the challenges his students face.

Paul's undergraduate degree in architecture did not have a lot of obvious relevance to teaching children; however, he feels his work experience "helped because I had a job where things were complicated and changed a lot. You're always talking with people and communicating. With architecture obviously there's a lot of creativity and invention, so I could transfer those skills to teaching." Paul was fairly positive about his one-year pre-service program where he received his credential to teach Kindergarten through grade 6, although he did note some shortcomings. The cohort program he chose was

> focused on inner-city schools, it was definitely tailored to that demographic. I got a lot of great ideas about books and resources that have been really useful. I got suggestions for how to structure things so as to be flexible and responsive to the students' backgrounds.

He found his two practice teaching placements helpful, one in grade 2 and one in a combined grade 4/5/6 class (in an alternative school). He wished his pre-service program had focused more on assessment and on theories of how children develop as readers and writers. He also felt some of the assignments were "busy work."

Description of Practice

At the heart of Paul's practice is a commitment to helping his students succeed. Attention to equity, diversity, and developing an inclusive community are the foundation of his work as a teacher, not simply "addons" to his program. He defines diversity broadly as including race, gender, class, and academic ability. Paul's own experience of racism growing up, his reading on social justice, and his involvement in a support group for Gay, Lesbian, and Transgendered parents have given him in-depth understanding of many related issues. His recognition of the links between education and overcoming societal barriers has led him to develop a program to help students acquire the knowledge, skills, and attitudes – in particular the self-esteem – to achieve in society and become involved citizens.

Believing that teaching is a relational act, Paul spends time getting to know his students: what is going on in their lives, their interests, anxieties, and strengths. "Teaching is a social skill; not just the performance aspect, but actually having relationships with people and developing those relationships." A natural extension of this position is to create a strong and safe class community. At the beginning of the school year he devotes time to community, using strategies such as daily sports activities, building Lego structures in groups, and talking about community. Given the life context of many of the children, Paul wants the class to be a place where they can raise questions. He aims to build a high trust level with his students, which was evident when one of his students said to him: "Is it normal to want to punch your mom?"

> My reaction was not panicky, even though inside I'm going, Whoa! My reply was, "Well, that's an interesting question. Why don't we talk about that later on?" I think it's really important for kids to feel they can speak about things.

In designing his literacy program, Paul wants to make connections with the real world and help children see that literacy is all around them.

> School has to connect to their real world, even if it is violent. Our students are jaded in a way, they are immature but they're also too worldly. I find I need things that are real-world, high-interest. But it's hard to find those things because a lot are not appropriate for school, or not deemed appropriate. Most of the music these kids listen to you can't listen to at school. I find that weird in a way, because what does that mean? They come to school and everything they like to do – the games, the music – they are not allowed to do at school. I find it worrisome that school is becoming irrelevant to them. Is it becoming so removed from their "real life" that they don't care about it?

He finds using newspapers a good strategy to make literacy relevant: the variety of sections appeals to a range of interests, articles are short, and the pictures help with comprehension. With multiple copies of the paper available, students often sit in groups reading and discussing the paper. He described one such session and commented: "They had this appearance of adult men sitting around, reading the paper, chatting about politics and sports. It was kind of neat to see that." Paul finds that graphic novels help make text accessible to his students. His students use computers effectively and he often books the school computer lab for his class. He thinks students need to be computer literate if they are to have a chance to succeed.

Paul promotes inclusion in part through the books he uses in his literacy program. He reads aloud to his students every day, often from books that address issues of equity and diversity. One of the novels he read to his students was

The Jacket about a boy who accuses another boy of stealing, and the boy who gets accused happens to be Black. It's all about racism, internalized racism, etc. It was a really good book, short, easy to get into. And the kids were just on the edge of their seats. [A second book I read], *The Breadwinner*, is about a girl living in Afghanistan during the Taliban occupation. So again, it was really interesting, connected to the students.

Paul was introduced to many books dealing with race, class, and gender in his pre-service program and continues to use them: for example, *Are You a Boy or a Girl?*, *Deshawn Days*, *Dreamcatcher*, *Heather Has 2 Mommies*, *Let's Talk About Race*, *Sticks and Stones* (about Internet bullying), and *Zen Shorts*. He both reads aloud to students and encourages them to read on their own.

I had a girl who was very, very boyish and she read *Are You a Boy or a Girl?* I would see her reading it and she was processing it and going, Oh, it's okay that I'm not so girlish.

In addition to this literature-based approach, Paul discusses inclusion explicitly with students when they make racist or ethnocentric comments in the classroom. He said:

I know that's what they hear at home, that some families are really racist … so I don't feel I can change their beliefs right away; but I want to show them what's acceptable and that they can't get away with saying things like that in class.

Sometimes Paul teaches skills in discrete lessons and at other times integrated into content areas. From his first year of teaching, Paul has tended to blur curriculum boundaries. When doing a social studies unit on early civilizations, he integrates "reading, comprehension, research skills, writing, sentences, paragraphs, and writing reports." He believes linking skills and content makes the program more engaging while also allowing him to attend to the many official curriculum expectations. Paul is not a teacher who feels pressure to "get through the curriculum"; rather, he aims to increase his students' understanding and expand their horizons. He wants to introduce students to many genres (especially the boys who only want to read books about sports) and encourages them to be self-directed, motivated, and responsible for their learning. He spends countless hours searching the Internet and the library for resources. He feels that almost every resource has to be tailored for his students. He complains about some of the items on the standardized test he has to administer because they revolve around a story about a cottage. As he notes, most of his students have never been to a cottage and have no concept of "going to the cottage."

Part of Paul's understanding of diversity is awareness that the cultures of many of his students are fairly oral and that oral language can be a bridge to print.

> I started a storytelling club this year and I do storytelling with my kids. I realized that a lot of kids need to be able to speak clearly, put their ideas together, and *say* them before they can even put them down. If they can't string together a sentence orally they're probably not going to sit down and write a coherent sentence. For a lot of these kids, oral language is huge. You can tell them a story and they will remember so much, but they will read the story on paper and remember and understand much less.

Paul's Class in Action

There are nine in Paul's class for "learning disabled" students (the class he had in his third year) – all boys, some with severe behavior issues, three students from each of grades 4, 5, and 6. From the moment the children tumble through the doorway, energy fills the room. The classroom is fairly small, with desks arranged in groups, a sofa, large arm chairs, and workspaces. Paul notes that it takes his students a long time to complete a task and he works patiently with them.

The afternoon begins with a review of how to write a summary of a story. It is difficult for the group to focus but Paul gently reminds them to attend to the lesson. After a short lesson, the students read trade books, either *The Salamander Room* or *Demolition* (a non-fiction text on techniques for demolishing buildings). Some students choose to read independently while others read with a partner. Some sit at their desks, others on the sofa, and one student who is known to like to read on his own without being disturbed sits apart in one of the easy chairs. It is interesting to observe the students because the more-able ones help those struggling with decoding or comprehension.

The students reading *Demolition* so enjoy the book that they want to read beyond the assigned chapters, which Paul allows them to do. He chose the book because many of the government-subsidized units where the children live are being torn down: they are literally being demolished before the students' eyes. As they read, students talk about the apartments being ripped down, the noise, the dust, and their concern about where they will live.

After a recess break, the students continue writing their summaries. Some use the computer program Co-Writer, which speaks the text as it is being written and gives choices for words as the students begin to spell them. It is a very good program and the students like using it. As they complete their summaries, the students begin work on their art, which Paul is going to submit to the school-wide art fair. Some work on sketches, some start painting; they chat as they work, sharing materials and assisting each other. As the end of the school day nears, Paul helps the pupils organize their materials for home and tidy up. He reminds them, with a great deal of humor, to remember to return to school tomorrow! He lets students take home computer discs (CD-ROMs) for computer programs they like to use.

Final Thoughts

Over the three years, Paul's skills as a teacher have improved – for example, in program planning – but the challenges he faces on a daily basis have rarely ebbed. The needs of the children are so great and their behavior at times so extreme that teaching drains him, as it would any teacher. Without a doubt his students' literacy and social skills improve, but at what cost to him personally?

Paul may see himself as a role model for his students but we also see him as a role model for teacher educators. We recognize that his teacher education program, focusing on urban schools, supported the development of his teaching skills, introduced him to a wide range of resources, and helped him refine his vision for schooling. The marrying of pedagogy and vision helped him become a truly outstanding practitioner. However, teacher educators cannot take all the credit: Paul is a truly remarkable individual with distinctive life experiences, talents, and insights. Teacher education needs to continue to attract candidates like Paul, and the school system needs to support committed young professionals so they remain in teaching, keeping intact their vision for supporting "high-needs" youth.

> **CASE STUDY ACTIVITY: In small groups, discuss the case study generally, then consider the following questions.**
>
> • Paul often ignores or modifies the official curriculum because it does not match the needs of his students. What are your views on his approach?
> • Paul has sacrificed much of his personal life – working long hours, worrying about the students – over the past few years. Is this a realistic expectation for teachers? What advice would you give Paul?
> • What is your response to Paul's belief that teaching is a relational act?

- Paul has often taught classes where the majority of students are high needs. What are your views of streaming students (i.e., low-ability students in one class, high-ability in another)?

Problems of Inclusive Education

Despite the value and legitimacy of inclusive education, it is beset by a number of challenges.

1. **It is a difficult area to understand and address.** The personal, ethical, political, and cultural issues are very complex and need to be sifted through. You should enter on the path, of course, but you will have to tread carefully, seek feedback, and take courses and read widely in the area.
2. **Students often bring prejudices, stereotypes, and exclusionary practices to school,** and questioning these can appear to challenge the students' freedom and identity. Initially, trying to promote inclusion in the classroom can give rise to discord as students disagree with each other or with what we are proposing (Paley, 1992).
3. **Adopting inclusive attitudes can lead to tensions for students beyond the school.** As they move in an inclusive direction, you must help them find ways to maintain their sense of belonging in their home, neighborhood, and other settings where different views may be held.
4. **Teachers who wish to foster inclusion may face challenges within the school system.** For example, official curricula tend to focus on "academic" learning, making it difficult to find time to address personal, cultural, and political matters (Sleeter, 2005). Again, the common emphasis on ability grouping and withdrawal of "struggling learners" from the class can reinforce stereotyping, prejudice, and exclusion of students from full membership in the class community.
5. **Teachers often lack experience of diverse settings and understanding of issues of inclusion and exclusion.** Though teachers are typically very sympathetic, you may not have much background or education in this area, and may have prejudices and stereotypes of your own.

ACTIVITY: During the Academic Program

- Working in groups, talk about one aspect of your background that makes you unique. Then consider ways in which all of you are similar. How can you learn about both differences and commonalities without becoming intrusive or making others feel uncomfortable? How can you apply this to your work as a teacher?

- Brainstorm a list of differences you would typically find in a classroom (e.g., gender, race, culture, sexual orientation). Recognize that pupils are always part of more than one group. Discuss how the differences could impact on individual students both positively and negatively. What would you do as a teacher to ensure that all pupils feel included?
- Discuss to what extent in teaching subjects (e.g., mathematics, science) you should follow an inclusive approach. As you do this, to what extent should you follow the official curriculum?
- What are some of the challenges of building community in a diverse classroom?
- How would you respond to students who hold highly sexist or racist views?

Principles and Strategies of Inclusive Education

Teachers cannot single-handedly cure society's ills, but you can do much to promote inclusion in your own classroom. Here are some relevant principles and strategies that we have taken from the research literature and from the new teachers in our study.

1. Emphasize Community

Students are strongly influenced by the views of their peers and what they see practiced in their classroom, and this applies in particular to matters of inclusion. As Linda Kroll at Mills College said in an interview:

> If you're going to talk about issues of social justice, equity, and excellence and have hard conversations about things like race and discrimination and how you feel about those things, then you have to have a safe place to talk about it. And if you are going to take risks, showing that you don't know something, there has to be a safe place. So ... the first thing you have to do is establish a community in your classroom where people feel free to say what they think.
>
> (Beck & Kosnik, 2006, p. 73)

Although Kroll was speaking here primarily about the pre-service context, the same argument applies to the school setting. If pupils are to think and speak freely about issues of inclusion and "try out" inclusive behavior, there has to be genuine community in the classroom.

Nearly all the new teachers in our study were teaching in schools with a wide diversity of race, ethnicity, economic circumstances, and academic attainment. A major strategy used to achieve and teach inclusion in this context was building class community. Wanda said she worked at

> creating community, because the biggest issue is getting the children to understand that their uniquenesses are fabulous, but we also need to draw on each other's strengths so we can support each other's weaknesses and create a sense of community.

Jeannie commented:

> I talk a lot about respect – it's actually a school-wide focus – and in September especially I do a lot of activities around it. And I model it: if there is name-calling, I stop the class and address it. And in the read-alouds I talk about bullying, teasing, and so on ... and about recognizing people's differences and accepting them.

ACTIVITY: For Your Resource Kit

Begin to locate books and films that address various aspects of diversity. Record the titles, authors, and source information.

2. Get to Know Your Students Well

The teacher–student relationship is crucial for teaching generally and especially for inclusive education. Teachers have to set the tone, showing that they respect all the students equally and are genuinely interested in getting to know them all. Martin (1992) maintains that school should be a place where students feel "safe, secure, loved, at ease ... 'at home'" (p. 12). It should be characterized by "affection ... intimacy and connection" (p. 18).

Among our new teachers, Wanda observed: "I can't say how I'm going to approach anything until I get to know the kids. And I think this is really important, both as a person and as a teacher." Carrie made a poignant comment about the need for a supportive teacher–student relationship:

> I've done more around acceptance of difference this year (year 3) than last year, and also encouraging students to believe in their abilities and accept themselves.... My brother has a learning disability

and probably my dad does too. So it's always been a core thing with me, that you learn differently, it's not that you can't learn … and you've got a right to an education. And also as a child myself I saw what it means to a kid when a teacher condemns them and doesn't support them.

3. Individualize the Program

If we are to show respect toward all the children in our class, we have to allow them to develop their own interests and use their distinctive learning styles. Among our study participants, one reported that in trying to make the topic of "medieval times" meaningful for her students she often departs from traditional content to a degree, giving illustrations from the medieval history of the non-European cultures represented in her class. Nina commented:

> [W]hen you teach a lesson you have to think about every child, you can't just teach in one way; for example, you have to ask yourself whether this child is going to understand the language, or whether that child has to move around a lot.

Anna spoke of the need to identify gaps in students' background knowledge and give them as much exposure as possible to information and experiences to help fill the gaps. Many described how they modify the program for ELL students (English Language Learners). In this connection, Felicity said: "It's just social justice, really … all these children should be given opportunities."

Sleeter (2005) says that allowing for "diversity in expertise" can prepare students for "participation in a multicultural democracy and diverse world" (p. 7). In relation to curriculum planning, she comments:

> It is the teacher's responsibility to find out, become familiar with, and respect the knowledge students bring to school, and to organize curriculum and learning activities in such a way that students are able to activate and use that knowledge.
>
> (p. 106)

---

4. Study Diverse Cultures

Studying different cultures – their distinctive ideas, customs, and achievements – is a major aspect of inclusive education (so long as we avoid the dangers of stereotyping). It increases respect for people who come from these cultures and provides a basis for seeing similarities between groups. Many of the new teachers emphasized that such study is an important foundation for mutual understanding and respect in the classroom. Felicity commented:

> We did a lot of diversity studies [in the pre-service program] and although I haven't done enough of it this year, because it's been too hectic, I really want to be the kind of teacher who perceives literature that's not mainstream, that's diverse.... It's really important that the students see themselves reflected in the literature, or see other cultures reflected in it, not just the mainstream one.

Maria reported:

> One of my girls found a book on Islam and she said, "This is my religion, Miss G"; and I said, "I know, go ahead and read it." So I try to select books that reflect the diversity in the class, and we talk about it, mainly during literacy.

Anita observed:

> This class likes [to learn] about different cultures, they're very interested in Chinese culture, African culture, and so on, so I bring those things in. For example, at Christmas time we talked a lot about Kwanza, and although nobody in the class celebrates Kwanza we talked about it anyway. Actually ... holiday time in December is a nice time to talk a lot about the festivals of different cultures, and the students really like it.

5. Support Students in Developing their Individual Way of Life

Students vary greatly in how much they wish to adhere to their heritage culture (and often they belong to several). Teachers need to be aware of this and talk with the students about conflicts that may arise between cultural traditions and individual needs, and how these conflicts might be addressed. Home and local cultures, just like dominant ones, can be authoritarian and limiting in certain respects. As a teacher you must help your students to *both* understand, value, and draw on their home and local culture(s) *and* develop an identity and way of life distinctly their own.

The importance of linking to students' own life was a recurring theme in the new teacher interviews. Candice gave as her "philosophy on literacy learning" that students should "be encouraged from where they are; it should be exciting, and they should see how it matters in their day to day life." Anita recalled learning in her pre-service program "the theory of how to facilitate kids talking about books and figuring out the parts they enjoyed and making the experience enjoyable for them." She spoke of "connecting to the things [students] read personally, relating things to the real world, their interests, and their lives."

6. Discuss Issues of Prejudice and Discrimination Explicitly

Although we believe inclusive education should largely be "infused" into the academic program, the life of the classroom, the teacher–student relationship, and the study of diverse cultures, there is definitely a place for explicit, critical discussion of issues of inclusion. Even in elementary school, students should begin to learn about the history and mechanisms of discrimination and how widespread it is in society. They should come to see how popular culture is pervaded by ideology and molded by the interests of dominant groups. However, these topics should be addressed in a sensitive manner within a supportive class community.

Many of our study participants saw the importance of explicit discussion in this area. Nina reported that she discusses racial and cultural diversity with her students and, in particular, the inappropriateness of linking race and national identity. Paul spoke of the need for explicit attention to problems of stereotyping, including self-stereotyping:

> In my school a lot of teachers focus on citizenship, values, and that kind of thing … because there are a number of students whose main barrier to any kind of learning is their attitude, the way they interact, their approach. For instance, there are boys who feel that being smart is not for boys, it's a girl thing. So reading books, oh well, you shouldn't do that if you're a guy because it's not cool.… And I think you have to teach them that people should do what they're good at, they should work on that.

ACTIVITY: During Practice Teaching

- Take a walk around the neighborhood of your practice teaching school. Note the housing conditions, types of stores, local community centers, and so on. What insights are you getting into the community? Your students?
- Before beginning your practice teaching, look at the school profile on the school or district website. Does the profile provide information about the make-up of the student

population? Do a little research on the backgrounds (e.g., culture) of your students so that you are better informed.

- As you teach, note the amount of time you spend talking to males versus females. Do you tend to give more attention to one group? Does one group tend to dominate discussions?
- If some of your students attend special classes or programs (e.g., ELL, Special Education), spend a morning or afternoon in these classes to get a better sense of what goes on. Note whether students act differently in these programs than in your classroom. Why the difference?
- Ask your cooperating teachers about the students in the class who are "special needs." Find out how the program is modified for them. Ask about the process for having a pupil tested and admitted to a special program.
- If your practice teaching schools are in high-needs areas, find out what kinds of support and outreach the school and district have for the community.
- Look at the explanation of complexity in the Introduction to this book. How does it apply to inclusive education?
- If your school has a Parent Council (i.e., for parents, school administrators, and teachers), attend one of the meetings to get a sense of how the school works with the community.

Conclusion

In the past, the term "inclusive education" has been used in a rather narrow sense to refer to the mainstreaming of "special education" students in regular classrooms. In line with growing practice, we use the term here much more broadly to refer not only to accommodating academic difference but also to being sensitive to differences of gender, class, race, ethnicity, language, physical ability, and so on. Such teaching is necessary (a) to optimize the learning of all pupils, whatever their abilities, interests, and background, and (b) to help pupils understand the nature of prejudice and discrimination, and acquire inclusive attitudes and behaviors.

Clearly, inclusive education is not just a frill or political nicety; it is fundamental to a constructivist pedagogy that strives to meet the needs and build on the experiences of all students. It is inherent in the respectful, dialogical, individualized, communal approach to teaching we have discussed so far in this book. However, attention must be given to the *manner* in which inclusive education is promoted. Rather than imposing it top-down, you should model it in the classroom and use dialogical methods to encourage your pupils to take personal ownership of an inclusive approach to their fellow students and in their life generally.

Chapter 5

Subject Content and Pedagogy

As a teacher, you will be responsible for teaching a great deal of content to your students. If you teach in the elementary grades, you will likely be teaching many subjects. At the high school level, you will help students acquire in-depth knowledge in specific areas. Regardless of grade or subject, your goals should be to help students learn important content and develop a positive attitude to the subjects they are studying.

Preparation to teach in specific subjects is essential (Ball, 2000; Hagger & McIntyre, 2006), yet not all teacher education programs give sufficient attention to subjects. It is important to emphasize subject content and pedagogy for the following reasons.

- School systems are subject oriented: you will spend most of your day teaching subjects.
- You can in fact teach a lot about important social issues and life skills through subject teaching, provided you are careful in the topics you emphasize and how you approach them.
- Learning certain subjects is a major aspect of learning about culture.
- Much subject knowledge is very interesting to students.
- Teaching subjects well is one of the main factors in effective classroom management.

PERSONAL ACTIVITY

What subject(s) are you very comfortable teaching? What subject(s) are you uncomfortable teaching? What subject makes you uncomfortable? Did you have a negative experience with this subject or subjects when you were a student or are you just not that interested in the content? How do you think your feelings about certain subjects will influence your teaching? You may have a degree in ancient history but be required to teach a more recent period of history. What do you need to learn to teach your subject(s) effectively?

What Subject-Specific Knowledge Do Teachers Need?

Teachers need to know both *subject content* and *subject pedagogy*. These two types of knowledge, taken together, are often referred to as "pedagogical content knowledge" (Ball, Thames, & Phelps, 2008; Shulman, 1986, 2004). Here we illustrate the two types by reference to literacy teaching.

1. The *subject content* teachers need in literacy includes:

    -   knowledge of genres (e.g., non-fiction, realistic fiction, fairy tales, drama, poetry, graphic novels, film, e-mail correspondence, weblogs, text messages);
    -   personal experience, enjoyment, and appreciation of various genres;
    -   knowledge of specific works of adult literature, children's literature, and young adult literature;
    -   knowledge of why people read and write;
    -   knowledge of the processes used in reading (e.g., drawing on phonemic awareness, activating prior substantive and vocabulary knowledge) and writing (e.g., having a sense of audience, finding one's voice as a writer).

2. The *subject pedagogy* teachers need in literacy includes:

    -   knowledge of "ways of representing and formulating" literacy that are especially powerful in deepening pupils' understanding and appreciation of it (Shulman, 2004, p. 203);
    -   awareness of which genres, works, topics, and themes within literacy are of most interest to pupils;
    -   familiarity with the typical blocks and misunderstandings pupils experience in relation to the literacy – "what kinds of errors or mistakes students are likely to make" (Grossman & Schoenfeld, 2005, p. 205);
    -   knowledge of especially effective methods for teaching literacy in the classroom;
    -   knowledge of child development and cultural backgrounds in relation to literacy: for example, the typical "learning progressions" (Shepard et al., 2005, p. 280) of children and "the conceptions and preconceptions that students of different ages and backgrounds bring with them to [literacy] learning" (Shulman, 2004, p. 203);
    -   knowledge of available textbooks, published programs, and other learning materials in the field of literacy (Shulman, 2004, pp. 203–204).

Wanda's Approach to Subject Content and Pedagogy: A Case Study

> My philosophy [of literacy teaching] is making sure that I have a lit-
> eracy rich classroom environment and that I'm giving these children
> every opportunity to be exposed to literacy. Whether it's the books
> they take home, the information here in the classroom, or even just
> the dialogue about reading, I am trying to teach them that reading
> is good, literacy is good, and it's fun.

Background

Wanda came to teaching as a second career, having spent 16 years in
the financial sector managing pension funds. Her undergraduate degree
was in economics and political science and she completed an MBA in
finance. She is a mother of three, has traveled extensively, and has lived
abroad. After her years in business, where she achieved considerable
success, she returned to university and gained her teaching credential
specializing in kindergarten through grade 6. Although she has been
actively involved in her own children's schooling, she noted in her third
year of teaching that "teaching is definitely a much tougher job than I
ever imagined it to be." Since being certified, she has taught in two different urban schools, initially teaching a combined grade 1/2 class and
then grade 2/3 classes in her second and third years. Because of a lack of
openings, she has yet to be granted a "regular" contract by the school
district and so has no job security.

Not surprisingly, given her initial career path, Wanda's undergraduate and previous graduate degrees were not related to teaching young
children, but she felt her work in the business world helped her because
"you learn how to talk to people, you learn how to have empathy, and
that's the key." Her experience in pension fund management was one of
the reasons she decided to drastically change her professional life and go
into teaching. When working with clients, she realized that many people
who had to make decisions about their own pensions had only func-
tional literacy, which led her to conclude that there is "something wrong
with the education system."

At first, Wanda was not enthusiastic about her teacher education
program, but as time went on she identified aspects that had influenced
her. Her two literacy instructors she described as "incredible." She
noted that "they took almost every opportunity to show how a book
could be used to introduce a topic or drive a lesson." They introduced
the students to publishers and a range of resources. She also completed
the optional training in Tribes, which she found very helpful, and she
continues to use many community-building strategies learned in the

pre-service program. Her two practice teaching placements – in grades 3 and 6 – did not seem to her to be particularly strong. The former was a very structured program and the latter she thought actually inhibited learning. Nevertheless, she felt "practice teaching was extremely useful, just because it puts you in a real-life situation."

Description of Practice

Wanda does not approach literacy as a series of subjects (e.g. spelling, writing, grammar); rather, her entire program has literacy at the core. She has reading and writing workshops; reading is often the spring-board for writing; she aims to build self-esteem in her students as readers and writers; there are extended periods for reading and writing every day; she integrates literacy into other subject areas (e.g., *A Clock for a Dreamer* to introduce a geometry unit); students learn develop-mentally appropriate strategies for reading and writing (e.g., picture clues for emergent readers); students can respond to texts in many dif-ferent ways (e.g., through visual arts); children are invited to talk about their learning and their preferred learning style; students participate in literature circles; and students have considerable choice in reading materials, and writing topics and activities.

The range of materials in Wanda's classroom is extensive – leveled books, high-quality children's books, non-fiction texts, multiple copies of the same book, books at different reading levels, books on tape, books by the same author – all beautifully displayed, accessible to the children, and well used. Central to Wanda's practice are her literacy centers. The children work often at the centers (making words, listen-ing, writing, doing guided reading) and she changes the centers regu-larly. Being a parent, she understands the importance of the school–home connection and finds ways to involve parents. She has established a Borrow-a-Book program and, recognizing that many parents do not speak English (but have home computers), she encour-ages them to use CD-ROMs with their children because they have pic-tures and voice-over.

Wanda aims to get to know each child individually, finding out his or her interests and strengths.

> The reality is that everybody learns at their own pace. In order to have a successful program, you have to insure there is solid ground-ing in the basic principles of literacy. And in order for a child to be successful, they have to like what they're doing. As a teacher, I have to try not so much to teach a child as to create an environment that makes it so enjoyable the child will want to read, learn, and con-tinue to question and grow. And that is very individual. Different

children have different needs and interests. So [I have] to be able to [develop] a program that's going to appeal to more than just one style of learner: not just one type of literature, it has to be a mixture of everything.

She uses a variety of class configurations – whole-class, small-group, and individual – matching them to the goals of the lesson. Her groups are fluid, sometimes heterogeneous and sometimes formed according to ability.

Wanda is required to use the DRA reading assessment system but she supplements it with her own data gathering in order to find out more about the children. "Assessment is not just black and white. There's going to be a lot of gray." She observes the children, listens to them read, holds individual writing conferences, talks to them about their learning, and sets clear goals for each unit that she shares with the children. Wanda does not want to simply assign a mark; rather, she wants to understand what the child has actually learned.

Sources of Learning

We were particularly interested to find out how Wanda had acquired such deep knowledge of literacy and literacy teaching, given that her pre-service program included only one course in this area. With her business background, there was not an obvious prior link with literacy. In some of the interviews we included questions specifically on sources of professional learning.

I. Own Experience as a Reader and Writer

Wanda emphasized that she is a reader and writer. "I love books, I love reading. And that was something that was always very strong within my own upbringing and about who I am as a person. My husband and I both love reading, so that's there." Valuing reading and writing in her personal life and understanding herself as a reader and writer were the foundations for her development as a literacy teacher.

2. Influence of Family

Wanda's family played a key role in the teacher she became. Teaching was part of her mother's family tradition.

My mother was a teacher for five decades and she was my mentor in this respect. If I could, I would model myself after her. Up until she died, she constantly had either former students or their parents coming up to her and basically thanking her for what they gained from her. She ended her career in Special Education; she always used to say that every child can learn, they just need to be given the time and the approach to learn.

When Wanda secured her first teaching position, she turned to her family for help, in particular a cousin who was a retired curriculum consultant.

She came in a couple of weeks before school, we set up the class-room, she had a substantial number of resources. She also had a friend, a primary years consultant who had just retired, and I got a lot of her resources as well. We laid out a plan of attack for my first month or two.

Working with her own children provided first-hand experience with lit-eracy. Her two older daughters were always keen readers but her son was a reluctant reader who would have rather played video games than read a book. Enticing him into reading helped her learn strategies for engaging children in her class.

3. Influence of a Model School

Wanda's first teaching position was in what was deemed a model liter-acy school. The principal was a true curriculum leader and the in-school Literacy Coordinator became Wanda's informal mentor. The school engaged in school-wide literacy initiatives. For example, February was poetry month, which meant that the whole school focused on poetry, poets visited the school to talk about being poets and writing poetry, staff attended workshops on writing poetry, and the school celebrated the children's poems. When the entire faculty adopted Lucy Calkins' approach to writing, teachers in division teams decided what forms of writing they would focus on. Teachers worked in grade teams to develop common curriculum expectations, review their approach to assessment, and plan teaching activities. Although each teacher was allowed flexibility in the strategies used, there was a consistent philo-sophy of literacy learning throughout the school. The principal provided many outside learning opportunities as well; for example, the school was chosen as one of 17 schools to visit New York City to observe exemplary literacy programs. Fortunately, Wanda's own views of reading and writing resonated with the philosophy advocated in this school, and this allowed her to advance her knowledge of literacy cur-riculum, pedagogy, and assessment. She spoke very highly of the experi-ence and regretted having to leave the school.

4. Professional Learning

Wanda truly took control of her learning and capitalized on everything that was offered. Before entering the teacher education program, she volunteered for over 200 hours in a primary teacher's classroom. The teacher, who had been a cooperating teacher for many years with a pre-service program, had an outstanding literacy program, and was a strong mentor. Wanda spent substantial time reading professional literature. On her own initiative, she read Debbie Miller, Sharon Taberski, Lucy Calkins, Irene Fountas, Gay Su Pinnell, and Patricia Cunningham. She acquired an extensive collection of teacher resource books, often spending her own money to purchase them. When she left her first school she remained on the listserv of the Literacy Coordinator, which allowed her to access the school district internal literacy website. She identified a grade 3 teacher in the district who had a website where he described his literacy centers. "I've been looking through his website as fast as I can to get ideas." Wanda enrolled in summer workshops in areas where she felt she needed to strengthen her program (e.g., science and art). She also completed an in-service course on special education.

Wanda's Class in Action

Entering Wanda's combined grade 2/3 class was enchanting. The classroom was old but bright. Books were everywhere but well-organized, children's work was on display, charts were hung across the room, motivational posters decorated the walls, one of the reading centers had stuffed animals, and desks were organized in groups. Although the group of children Wanda taught in her third year were particularly challenging, she truly cared for each student and worked patiently with all.

When students entered the class, they immediately focused on organizing their agenda, homework, money for the pizza lunch, and so on. Once this "housekeeping" was done, students began to read silently. Some wandered over to the literacy corner and curled up with a stuffed animal, some read in pairs, others stayed at their desks. Most were engrossed in their reading. After about 20 minutes of reading, Wanda gathered the students to continue working on their novel. They reviewed the events from *Stone Fox* before she began to read aloud; during and after the reading, they discussed the events. Wanda's questions probed the motives of the characters and the impact of events on them. As a follow-up writing activity, students had to write a journal entry from the perspective of one of the characters, describing how he or she was feeling about the events that had just occurred. For about 20 minutes, students worked on their writing, obviously comfortable with the task, using invented spelling and sharing their work with each other. When they reconvened on the carpet, some students read their work aloud, with Wanda commenting on the strengths of each piece.

After recess, the class had a science lesson. They had been studying soil and started the lesson with a review of why some of the class plants had flourished and others had not. Wanda then formed random groups for a game of Jeopardy focused on soil. The students had previously written questions and answers for the game. There was lots of laughter and enthusiasm for the game. The students understood the concepts, having recently completed a project on an animal that lives underground. Wanda had read them *Diary of a Worm*, and they had to research an animal or insect of their choice that lives in the soil and do a diary entry for it.

Final Thoughts

Wanda is an interesting case because she has acquired a great deal of knowledge outside her teacher education program. At the heart of Wanda is an insatiable desire to learn; whether she is in the business world or in education, she is a learner. Admittedly she is unusual in that she seems to have an innate understanding of reading and writing processes. However, she has not simply relied on her natural talent: she spends countless hours learning both theory and practical strategies. Actually, we worry that Wanda is setting the bar too high. In our interviews, she talked about the substantial time she devotes to planning her program (e.g., acquiring suitable texts and searching the Internet for lessons or resources). In her first year of teaching, she often spent most of Saturday and Sunday planning lessons and units, and we are not sure her planning time has decreased substantially since then. But if in the future Wanda has to ease up a bit, in the interests of personal well-being, it is clear she will continue to learn and be an outstanding teacher.

The influence of the model literacy school in Wanda's first year shows the potential of immersing a novice teacher in such a setting. She had many opportunities to learn, was able to observe good practice, and had support in building her program:

> The staff worked as a community, I was exposed to so much. It was just the wealth of knowledge they had. Their approach was very holistic in terms of looking at a child and trying to figure out how to approach the learning for him or her.

Such an experience would be ideal for all beginning teachers and in turn would have enormous benefit for pupils.

CASE STUDY ACTIVITY: In small groups, discuss the case study generally, then consider the following questions.

- How did Wanda increase her knowledge of literacy teaching? What professional development opportunities (e.g., conferences, websites, journals) are available to you in your local area?
- What are some strategies Wanda used to motivate pupils?
- Teachers cannot be experts in every subject. What are some of the challenges teachers face when they don't know enough about a subject they have to teach? How can they deal with this situation?
- Wanda's love of reading influenced her practice. What hobby or interest do you have that facilitates your work as a teacher?

Problems of Acquiring Knowledge of Subject Content and Pedagogy

Although the need is clear, it is difficult for teachers to acquire enough knowledge of subject content and pedagogy. Here are some of the obstacles you may face.

1. Lack of time in pre-service and in-service programs to study subject content and pedagogy in the depth needed.
2. In your previous education, you may not have studied subjects in the manner needed for teaching.
3. You may have little or no undergraduate background in one or more of your main teaching subject(s).
4. Sometimes, pre-service faculty are also patchy in their knowledge of subject content and pedagogy.

Without sufficient subject knowledge, the challenge of enactment discussed in the Introduction takes on greater significance. It is very difficult to teach a particular curriculum or establish a positive class community if your subject teaching is dry and superficial; pupils will tune out.

ACTIVITY: For Your Resource Kit

Ask your professors/instructors about professional organizations. Check out the websites of these groups to find out about conferences, books, and professional development opportunities. Bookmark the sites. Print off the home page of various subject organizations and file the pages in your Resource Kits under the appropriate subject. Consider joining an organization; many have student rates (e.g., Association for Teachers of Mathematics, www.atm.org.uk/).

Principles and Strategies Related to Subject Content and Pedagogy

There are a number of challenges, then, in preparing to teach subjects. However, we believe progress can be made in overcoming these challenges if teachers have a clearer understanding of the subject-specific knowledge they need, why they need it, and how they might acquire it. We now discuss several principles and strategies in this area. As in other chapters, we draw on both the research literature and our own research on new teachers.

1. Be Selective About Subject Content and Learning Activities

The first point to recognize is that not all content is equally relevant and interesting to students. As we saw in Chapter 1, we have some leeway in choosing which topics to emphasize and how to teach them. We should use this choice to make subject learning as engaging and worthwhile as possible, both for a whole class and for particular students. Here is an interesting example of how teachers exercised their choice in subject teaching. Darling-Hammond, Banks, Zumwalt, Gomez, Sherin, Griesdorn, and Finn (2005) describe how two English classes, both studying the same text (Sophocles' *Oedipus the King*), had extensive differences in approach.

a. "In one group, the teacher assigns the reading of the book as homework, holds two days of discussion about the book in class, and has students take a test on the book emphasizing new vocabulary and facts about characters and plot details" (p. 182).
b. "In the other group, the teacher provides a choice of essay questions, such as 'Was Oedipus a victim of fate or did he create his own destiny?', a month in advance. She begins the unit with a contemporary essay about the Oedipus complex, relating this common term to what students are about to read. They read the book over two weeks, combining daily read-alouds and dramatic presentations of the play with nightly reading for homework and guided journal questions.... Class discussions in large and small groups take up these questions.... The class also stages a debate on the question of Oedipus' responsibility for

his fate; students then write a series of drafts regarding the essay question chosen, with peer review and teacher review before completing a major essay on the book."

(p. 182)

2. Develop Goals as a Basis for Selecting Content and Pedagogy

In order to select appropriate subject content and activities, you must have a sense of your main goals as a teacher, as discussed in Chapter 1. "Covering the curriculum" is not an adequate goal for teaching. You need to identify "big ideas" about what is important for your students.

Several of the participants in our study spoke of the need to have goals for selection of content and activities. For example, Anita said we should ask: "Okay ... what are the main skills students need to know in, say, the context of science that will take them forward in their learning?" Felicity reported:

> Previously I tended to be eclectic – teaching interesting bits and pieces here and there – or perhaps chaotic might be a better word. But now [year 3] I'm becoming more coherent, which is exciting: I think my teaching will improve with that approach.

In the field of literacy, your broad goals for students might include:

- enjoying reading and writing of particular kinds;
- being able to select and read books independently;
- being able to comprehend text, discuss it with others, and write about it;
- being able to write for particular audiences;
- relating what one is reading to contemporary issues and one's own life;
- being critical of various media products;
- appreciating the aesthetic aspects of reading and writing;
- being comfortable with information and communication technology.

As you develop and refine such goals, you must keep in mind the ultimate purposes of education for students and society.

3. Integrate Subject Teaching

An important principle for selection of subject content and activities is integration of subjects – e.g., literacy, math, technology – "across the curriculum." Integration of subjects serves many purposes:

a. relating subject study more closely to the real world;
b. increasing the depth of learning;
c. covering more material;
d. increasing the level of interest.

Many of the participants in our study stressed the need to integrate subjects. Marisa, although clearly in favor of teaching individual subjects well, took a strong stand against having specialist subject teachers in elementary school.

> I don't think it matters whether [an elementary teacher] is a specialist or not.... I can learn [the content] and apply it in my class.... My fear is that if you have specialists they will teach using lectures and so on, and integration with other curriculum areas will be more difficult. This applies especially to kindergarten through grade 6; but I know some middle schools that are moving away from rotary because they're realizing that chunking the subjects is not effective.

ACTIVITY: During the Academic Program

• Discuss Marisa's beliefs that subjects should not be taught by specialist teachers in elementary and/or middle school. Do you agree? What are the benefits and limitations of having subject-specialist teachers?
• Describe an interdisciplinary learning activity (e.g., a field trip or making a video) in which students simultaneously learn (a) important subject content, (b) required "school" knowledge and skills, and (c) broader life insights and skills. What are the advantages of interdisciplinary work? What makes linking subjects challenging for new teachers?

4. Collaborate With Other Teachers in Subject Teaching

a. In the Same Grade or Division

Teaching subjects with colleagues can:

• increase integration;
• help with lesson preparation;
• make teaching more enjoyable;
• model a collaborative approach to inquiry and to activities generally.

Vera reported:

> [At our school], the grade 1 team sits down every week, and we bring our materials, what we've done in the past, what we've seen done, and our research on other programs. We decide what our focus will be and what we want to do; and then we copy and distribute it.

Deirdre and her teaching partner in New York City had a rocky first year, but in their second year resolved their differences and became a dynamic team who treasured working together.

b. Across the Whole School

As far as possible, collaboration in teaching subjects should occur throughout the school. In this way, students can get used to certain terms and methods; key concepts, principles, and skills can be taught in depth; and unnecessary repetition can be avoided. Margaret and Natalie's school had literacy and math coaches who organized whole-school initiatives and worked very effectively with all the teachers. Marisa commented:

> I think [collaboration] is extremely important, both within a division or grade but also school-wide. All teachers need to be speaking the same language – although of course you would modify that according to the students' level of understanding. For example, if you're teaching the elements of a story, everyone would call the events "events," or you might call it "plot": but it would be consistent right from kindergarten to grade 5 so it wouldn't confuse the kids. Also the types of resources would be the same, and ... even the type of graphic organizers we use should be consistent ... so the kids know exactly what to do. Having said that, we should know what writing forms are being taught in each grade so we don't repeat certain things and miss out on others.

5. Continue to Pursue Subject Matter Knowledge and Appreciation

As a teacher you must *yourself* continue to grow in subject knowledge and appreciation throughout your career. Too often, teachers see themselves as having already mastered their subjects, or as knowing so much more than their students that further learning is unnecessary. However:

- The *more* you know about the content of your teaching subject(s), the *higher* the likelihood that your teaching of that subject will be strong and engaging.
- You need to model for your students a continued fascination with a subject and strategies for ongoing learning.
- If you make continued learning a priority, your professional life will be more fulfilling. Instead of dreading having to "teach that again," you will approach each class with the attitude: "What new things do I have to offer today and what new things will I learn?"
- Deeper knowledge of your subject(s) will also greatly enrich your life *beyond* the school.

By their third year of teaching, many of the new teachers in our study saw the need for ongoing enhancement of their subject knowledge and appreciation. Anna spoke of the difficulty she had experienced teaching literacy because she "never loved literacy that much." Nina noted that to teach a subject well, "I have to make it interesting to me: if it's not interesting to me, I can't do it."

Marisa said that teachers must acquire "a broader picture of what math can be" so they can give up the typical "rule-based, rote-based" approach to math and show students that math can be done "in a variety of ways." Similarly, Anita gave an example of how she can now teach math better because she understands it better.

> [Over the past three years], I've learned how to multiply. When I was a kid I learned how to multiply, but when I learned it again I learned it in terms of place value, and now I really understand what it is and can teach it to my students.... And every year I'm still learning, because I have to learn the content before I can learn or develop strategies for teaching it.

With respect to enrichment of their own life, Karen said:

> Now that I'm teaching writing, I'm becoming a more active reader and also a better writer than I was before.... It's so stimulating! And sometimes when I'm reading to my daughter I'll say, "Oh my God, I've got to read this to the kids.... Wow, look at the way the author put those words together."... So yeah, I feel all the time that I'm developing as a teacher and as a person.

6. Continuing to Grow in Subject-Specific Pedagogical Knowledge

While subject *content* knowledge is clearly necessary for a teacher, subject-specific *pedagogical* knowledge is also essential. It has often been assumed that if you know the content you will be able to teach it, but that isn't necessarily so. Earlier we listed types of pedagogical knowledge you need as a teacher, such as subject-specific child development, teaching strategies, and school district programs. With respect to child development, several new teachers in our study said they needed to know more about stages of reading development; notably, how we can interest grade 4–6 students in reading, now that they have acquired the basics of decoding. Similarly, many said they wished they knew more about their school district's programs when they began teaching. Vera commented: "There are so many programs and materials out there it's hard to sift through them all and know which ones will work in your classroom." While graduates go to different school districts, there are broad trends and similarities in materials and programs that student teachers can come to understand.

As well as learning about subject-specific pedagogy during pre-service, student teachers should develop plans for *ongoing* learning in this area. What is learned in initial training is just the tip of the iceberg. As Tanya said:

> When I started, I didn't realize how little subject-specific knowledge I had.... And the more I learn, the more I realize how much I need to learn.... It takes a lot of dedication to get to the level you need, because you can certainly just come in and leave every day and get through just fine. But that's not the best way to do it.

You need the same attitude to subject pedagogy as to the subject itself: a passion to constantly learn more, both for your students' sake and your own. Within your school, you need to get together with other teachers to discuss materials and pedagogy. Vera noted:

> At my school we have an amazing in-service offering called the Curriculum Cafe, where we all get together for breakfast and people who have been at workshops present resources they have encountered and talk about them, telling us what is good, what is not, and how to use them. And I did this in my Reading Part 1 course as well: we all took a professional resource we had read and discussed what it stands for and how you can use it.

ACTIVITY: During Practice Teaching

- Spend time reading the student textbooks and the teacher resource guides. You can learn a tremendous amount from textbooks. Record the title of textbooks you think are good. Use the Internet to find more information on certain topics. Bookmark key sites.
- When planning your lessons, consider how much "punch" your lessons have. Are they dry? Are they just a recitation of facts and figures? Are you bringing some passion to the lessons? If you do not have enthusiasm, most likely your students will mirror your low level of interest.
- How can you make the content come alive? If possible, observe a few other expert teachers to see how they make their lessons engaging.
- As you look through the government-mandated curriculum documents, think about how you can link topics together in interesting ways.
- Talk to your associate teachers about the "big ideas" in particular subjects and topics.
- Look at the account of apprenticeship of observation in the Introduction. How does it apply to subject content and pedagogy?
- What hobbies or interests do you have that you can bring into your teaching?

Conclusion

As a classroom teacher you will be required to spend most of your time teaching specific subjects such as literacy, math, and science. Generally speaking, the more you know about these subjects – and specific ways of teaching them – the more interesting and effective your teaching will be. As well as knowledge of content, you need personal appreciation of subjects, the ability to select appropriate topics and activities within subjects, grasp of connections between subjects, understanding of "links to life," knowledge of subject-specific child development and teaching methods and materials, and the attitudes and behaviors necessary for ongoing development of subject-specific knowledge and appreciation.

Acquiring all this knowledge, appreciation, and skill requires an enormous amount of time. One way you can find more time is to combine subject-specific learning with learning about general educational issues and principles. Constructivism, program planning, assessment, inclusion, collaboration, and other key educational topics should to a large extent be studied in the context of studying subject-specific matters. An advantage of this approach is that the general topics will be understood more clearly because they will be illustrated in specific contexts. But no matter how effective your initial study of subject content and pedagogy may be, so much will remain to be learned. You need to embark on a life-long program of learning subject content and pedagogy, realizing that you will thereby greatly enhance your teaching and enrich your own life.

Chapter 6

Professional Identity

Each person who comes to teacher education has a conception of what it means to be a teacher. Having been in school for many years, you have developed a view of how teachers approach their work. Your long apprenticeship of observation (described in the Introduction) helped you construct an understanding of yourself as a teacher. A high priority in teaching is having a sound sense of your role as a teacher and how that role relates to the rest of your life. The whole person of the teacher is involved in the teaching–learning process: a teacher is not a mere "conduit" through which knowledge passes to the child (Connelly & Clandinin, 1999).

PERSONAL ACTIVITY

Teachers have an image of themselves as teachers. Having a sense of the type of teacher you want to be will guide your work. Take a few minutes to complete each prompt.

- The teacher I am ...
- The teacher I want to be ...
- The teacher I fear becoming ...

Consider ways that you can become the teacher you want to be. File this activity in your Resource Kit. Each year, re-read it to see how your view of yourself as a teacher is changing or staying the same. Keep updating your self-image as a teacher as you become more experienced and able to handle the challenges of enactment and complexity described in the Introduction.

Why is Professional Identity Important?

1. You need a broad professional self-image so that you can pursue all the goals necessary to be an effective teacher.

2. A broad and strong identity can give you greater pride in the profession and a more positive view of the contribution you make to your students' lives.

3. Developing your identity as a teacher can optimize the relationship between your professional and personal lives, enabling you to harness your personal interests and talents as you teach. As Hagger and McIntyre (2006) say: "Most teachers find that their individual humanity and the totality of their human experience are essential resources on which they draw as classroom teachers" (p. 55).

4. Developing your professional identity can add an important directional aspect to your career as you see yourself on a continuous path of professional growth, including – if you wish – new leadership roles in the school and beyond.

What is a Teacher's "Professional Identity?"

By "professional identity" we mean how you perceive yourself as a teacher: both your view of the role and how you connect to it personally. It includes your sense of your goals, responsibilities, style, effectiveness, level of satisfaction, and career trajectory. As a new teacher, your initial identity will come from a variety of sources: for example,

• memories of your own teachers when you were in school: the apprenticeship of observation (Lortie, 1975);
• internalization of societal views of the profession (Kennedy, 2005);
• prior notions about what you will be able to achieve, often based more on youthful optimism than experience and research.

As you engage in pre-service preparation and begin full-time teaching, you have the opportunity to develop your identity further. You do this by learning more about the possibilities and realities of teaching, and also making personal decisions about the kind of teacher you wish to be.

David's Sense of Professional Identity: A Case Study

When I started teaching First Aid courses, I was 18 years old and the kids I was teaching were 14. Not a lot of age difference there. I came in and tried to be this authority figure. Well, I'm only four years older than these kids and I'm sure when I walked in the door, they spotted a phony and to be perfectly frank, they ate me alive. It was a very long, dragged-out course. We got through it but in that course I learned a lot.

Background

After completing his Bachelor of Arts degree, David immediately entered a two-year teacher credential program. In the three years that followed (the period of our study), he taught grade 7 in a middle- to upper-middle-class suburban school with a high percentage of minority students. The school district is very large and quite traditional, and tends to be prescriptive with respect to curriculum teaching materials.

David was fairly positive about his teacher education program, although he felt there were too many "busy work" assignments. He found the courses on legal issues and assessment particularly helpful.

> I felt well prepared to be in the profession. I think two years is a very good idea in terms of preparation. The practicums obviously – doing four – make you confident in your own developing style as a teacher and what you're going to do in the classroom.

He did three of his four practicums in the school that eventually hired him, including one semester in grade 7 where he and his mentor teacher held similar views on literacy instruction. In his first year of teaching he based his program on the one he had experienced during his practicum. "I started off with a long-range plan from the teacher who taught this grade last year and who I worked with as a student teacher." During his pre-service program, David took a course on teaching English in middle school, but commented that it was not particularly helpful because the program advocated was not realistic for middle school students.

David's Identity as a Teacher

In our experience, it is rare to meet a beginning teacher as poised as David. He is self-assured, while recognizing he has much to learn. He cares about his students but has minimal classroom management issues. He focuses on pupil learning but also wants to foster a love of reading. His classroom is incredibly well-organized but he aims to build a community. Many might be challenged by these tensions but David in his pragmatic approach reconciles them as just part of teaching.

David takes his work as a teacher seriously. As he commented at the end of his third year: "Teaching is not a 9 to 5 job, you are a teacher all the time. It is fundamentally your life – inside and outside the classroom." He feels that one of the essential qualities for being an effective teacher is "whole-hearted commitment." Nevertheless, he sees the need for teachers to look after themselves – indeed, enjoy themselves – if they are to survive:

> There are times in this job when your principal is saying he needs such and such done; kids in the class are coming up and telling you they haven't done their homework; you've got a parent on the phone saying they don't understand the assignment and need more time; and you realize that it's May and in two weeks you have to start writing report cards. It's then that you need the ability to step back and just laugh.... [And] these kids, if you let them, will make you laugh, they will entertain you.... And you have to be able to enjoy yourself, otherwise you'll never get through it.

In defining himself as a teacher, David sees his job as ensuring success for all children: he strives to ensure that each student has a "personal best in grade 7." In all the interviews, he emphasized student learning, which he sees as his responsibility and as revolving around teaching the curriculum. Over time he feels less constrained by the formal curriculum expectations and the school district approved reading program, but he never strays far from a focus on teaching the curriculum.

While aiming at success for all students, however, David is realistic about what he can do. In the pre-service program, "I had more of a global idealism that I could change the world." This has been tempered by recognizing that not all children will have the same achievements. "My goal now ... is having every student ... learn at their level." In general, David is now more aware of the constraints on academic teaching. At the end of year 3, he commented:

> If there's one thing I would have liked to know about program planning it's that it doesn't come straight from the teacher's guide.... You have to look at it and say okay, in reality, what can I do? Because, for example ... my scheduled time for language arts is an hour, but by the time I start, it's quarter after, and then they have to do some seat work otherwise they're overloaded with homework. So you're talking about a 25 to 30 minute lesson. And one thing I've learned is that if I'm doing anything that's longer than 25–30 minutes, I should stop: for their sanity and mine. They're not going to absorb it, and I get panicked because I'm running out of time and start to speed up, and don't allow for questions.

David's identity as a teacher also includes being involved in all aspects of the school. He participates fully in the grade 7 and 8 divisional meetings, is on school-wide committees, is the union representative, and is very prominent in extra-curricular activities such as coaching. He believes that part of the reason parents respect him is his very visible presence coaching school teams.

Influences on David's Professional Identity

In studying David, we wanted to understand how a new teacher could have such a clear and strong sense of his professional identity. Over the three years, we noted three major influences.

1. Early Teaching Experiences

David is an extremely fit young man who has spent a lifetime involved in athletics. For over a decade he assumed different roles in aquatics programs where, in his view, he acquired many skills for teaching. "The first thing I started doing was teaching little ones how to swim. You have a basic curriculum, front floats, back floats, etc." This evolved into his becoming "a First Aid and National Life Saving Society instructor where you teach people who are becoming life guards the skills they need." He now has 38 different certifications. David's long-term and continued involvement in aquatics influenced him as a teacher: maintaining the discipline of athletic training, aiming for personal bests, teaching skills, and focusing on safety. His success in aquatics gave him confidence that he could teach and, as the opening quote indicates, many opportunities to refine the craft of teaching and develop his self-image as a teacher.

2. Apprenticeship in the School

David's three practicums as a student teacher in the school in which he was ultimately hired eased his transition into teaching. During practice teaching he established relationships with the teachers, in particular those teaching grades 7 and 8; they work as a team (e.g., developing a behavior code for all students) and they welcomed him onto the team even as a student teacher. "The support from the teachers is there. If I ask them a question I'll find an answer. But they don't say this is what you should do in terms of your literacy program, they don't micromanage in that way." In turn he feels he has influenced them by providing in-services on new curriculum documents, as we describe later.

David works closely with another new teacher who also teaches grade 7, splitting some teaching responsibilities; this eases the demands of program planning. When observing his class, we noted that this colleague wanders into the classroom and asks a question or figures out scheduling details (e.g., the time for an assembly). They have a very easy and collegial relationship. The Junior Literacy Coordinator helped David set up his program and hired him to be an instructor in the Summer Literacy Camp. He describes her as "a walking encyclopedia of literacy." In his first year, he said: "I'll tell her how I want to approach a unit and she'll fine-tune it, or give me some things to think about, or come back and say: That's good; can you take it to this level?" By the second year he was "more likely to try it on my own. If it didn't work, I would go back and say, okay, this is what I did, this is what happened; and then see what feedback she had for me." The various forms of mentorship improved his teaching, especially reducing the problems of classroom management that can undermine a beginning teacher's confidence.

3. Early Leadership Opportunities

Interestingly, David became involved in two major district-wide committees in his second year of teaching. This happened partly by chance: while attending a district-sponsored workshop, he was invited by one of the facilitators to join the committees. For one committee, he had to develop a working knowledge of the document *Think Literacy*, which focuses on comprehension strategies; he had to teach particular strategies to his class, collect samples of student work, and then lead in-services for teachers. On the second committee – the diversity writing team – he was required to develop curriculum for teaching a particular novel. (In addition, David was approached by a publisher to be a demonstration teacher for a video they were making of their new literacy program, and he was videotaped teaching literacy strategies to his class.) Doing professional development sessions for experienced teachers could have been daunting for a new teacher, but David was in a very supportive team environment. As the committees worked together conducting many in-service sessions, he began to see himself as a leader and teachers in turn saw him as leader. David knew early in his career that he wanted to be in educational leadership (he would like one day to become a principal); having a sense of his career trajectory, then, he welcomes these leadership opportunities because they match the vision he has for himself. He intends to complete his principal certification courses as soon as possible.

Beyond deepening his knowledge of curriculum, the committee work has introduced him to many outstanding teachers and consultants. He commented at the end of his third year that "disillusionment is a collective state of being for teachers." After ten years of school funding reductions and brutal attacks on teachers by the government in the media, there is a "collective pessimism." Through his leadership work, he has connected with many who have a brighter outlook toward teaching and higher morale. He thoughtfully commented: "If you are surrounded by negativity it is hard not to get snowballed into it." The networking let him "hear other voices and be introduced to educators doing other things," which has helped him retain his optimistic view of teaching.

David's Class in Action

David's grade 7 classroom is extremely well-ordered and tidy. There is student work on display; a chart with the code of behavior is prominently placed at the front of the room; homework notices are posted; and the furniture is arranged in a U-shape so everyone focuses on the front of the room. When the bell rings, the students enter the class and immediately turn their attention to getting organized for work. There is quiet chatting as they sort through their materials. In the first period, the language arts lesson involves reading a story about the adventurer John Goddard from the textbook *Sightlines*. Students take turns reading aloud, all are engaged, and many respond to questions posed by David. There is a quick review of strategies that can be used for synthesizing information and drawing inferences from text. Students then answer a question from the textbook, which requires them to identify three pieces of advice implied in the story of John Goddard and organize them in a paragraph. All students are on-task and work quietly for almost 30 minutes. The next period is history, and the class is studying a crucial era in early Canadian history. Again, the students use the textbook, with David reading the text and adding many fascinating details that help "history come alive." All the students are attentive and on-task. The history lesson is repeated after recess with the other grade 7 class.

Next Steps

David's experiences in teaching to date have been very positive, with a close match between his ideal and the reality, a sense that his pupils are learning, a feeling that he is respected by his colleagues, and many opportunities to exercise leadership. His view of the role of the teacher is in line with his pedagogy, classroom organization, and extra-curricular activities, thus creating a seamless practice.

David had planned to switch grades in his fourth year and teach a combined grade 5/6 class in the same school; however, while we were on-site during one of our year 3 visits he was offered a position in a local high school as a Career Path teacher, working with at-risk youth. He was extremely excited about this new challenge, recognizing that he would have much to learn. He was recently granted admission to a doctoral program on educational leadership but had to decline because of the high tuition cost. He intends to re-apply once he is in a better financial situation. It will be interesting to continue following David, a young man with great potential, a commitment to education, an optimistic yet realistic outlook, and a strong sense of direction in his career.

CASE STUDY ACTIVITY: In small groups, discuss the case study generally, then consider the following questions.

- How do you think David's early involvement in leadership activities is shaping his career?
- David has his career trajectory planned. What are the advantages and disadvantages of having such a specific plan?
- In terms of your career, where do you see yourself in five years? 10 years? 15 years? Do you consider teaching to be a long-term occupation for you?
- David felt that many of the assignments in his teacher education program were "busy work." What assignments are helping you become the teacher that you want to be? Can you modify any assignments (with agreement from your instructor) to help meet your needs?

Problems of Professional Identity

The professional identity of teachers is not a common topic in educational research and teaching. We were surprised to see how much emphasis was placed on it by the teachers in our study. The area deserves attention, not only because of its importance but because it is beset by a number of challenges.

- Teaching is usually defined far too narrowly.
- The intellectual depth and knowledge of teachers is often underestimated, despite the fact that they have at least one university degree. Because they work with children, they tend to be "infantilized" by the system and society (Barth, 1990, p. 36). (This is a sad commentary on society's view of children and also its simplistic conception of teaching.)
- Teachers are expected to be authority figures, distanced from their pupils, "the sage on the stage." This image is often supported by parents and even pupils themselves.
- Teachers often see themselves as "serving" students (as in other "helping professions"): self-sacrifice is a given.
- Initially, teachers tend to see themselves as "super-teachers," able to "work wonders" in children's lives (Kosnik, 1999).

ACTIVITY: During the Academic Program

Work in small groups to discuss the following questions.
- What do you think are the differences between approaching teaching as a job and approaching it as a profession?

- The public has many misconceptions about teachers, believing that teachers have a fairly easy life (e.g., long summer holidays, short work day). How do you think teachers can help the public appreciate the complexity of teaching?
- Teachers are portrayed in movies and books in a variety of ways (e.g., *Dead Poets Society*; *The Freedom Writers*; *Dangerous Minds*; *Stand and Deliver*; *To Sir, With Love*; *Teacher Man*). What are some of the common images of teachers? Are these realistic? How do these stereotypes help or hinder the profession? Have you seen a movie or read a book that you feel realistically portrays teaching?

Principles and Strategies of Professional Identity Formation

While it is important for you as a teacher to have a sense of identity, some self-perceptions are better than others. In this main section of the chapter, we discuss which elements of professional identity are most valuable for a teacher and how you might develop them further.

I. See Teaching in Broad Terms

Perhaps the most important thing to recognize about the teacher's role is that it is very broad: it goes far beyond just transmitting subject knowledge. As Mary Kennedy (2006) states, "teaching is a multifaceted activity … teachers routinely do more than one thing at a time" (p. 205). In fact, being able to "multi-task" is a prerequisite for being a teacher. In a recent study, Kennedy (2006, p. 205) found that teachers were concerned with the following:

a. covering desirable content;
b. fostering student learning;
c. increasing student willingness to participate;
d. maintaining lesson momentum;
e. creating a civil classroom community;
f. attending to their own cognitive and emotional needs.

To these we might add other important components, such as:

g. "assessing" students and listening carefully to their views;
h. individualizing instruction;
i. developing a good relationship with individual students;
j. attending to the values and "literacies" of the home and community;
k. helping students explore life issues and build their "way of life."

ACTIVITY: During the Academic Program

- Discuss the above list. Are there items you would add or ones you would delete as being of lesser importance?
- How do the lists above support the argument that two of the major challenges faced by new teachers are complexity and enactment (as described in the Introduction)? To what extent does knowing about these two challenges – and the breadth of your role – better prepare you to be a teacher?

The new teachers in our study increasingly saw the need for a broad teaching role and seemed willing to accept it as part of their professional identity. For example, Wanda commented that "teaching is no longer just knowing subject matter; it's also knowing psychology, and social work, and classroom management, and peer management techniques: how to work with colleagues."

2. Be Realistic About the Challenges of Teaching

David Labaree (2004) says: "[T]eaching is an extraordinarily difficult form of professional practice. It is grounded in the necessity of motivating cognitive, moral, and behavioral change in a group of involuntary and frequently resistant clients" (pp. 55–56).

Those who suggest that teachers have an easy time of it because of their "short work day" and summer break have no understanding of the reality.

- Students can be resistant.
- The actual work day is in fact long.
- The work is so hard that most teachers feel drained at the end of the day and week.
- Facilities and resources are often inadequate.
- External control measures often run counter to sound teaching.
- Constant uninformed criticism comes from many quarters.

You need to acknowledge and come to terms with all these challenges as you forge your professional identity.

Among our study participants, Felicity at the end of her second year said she continued to find teaching very demanding.

Teaching is a lot harder than I thought it would be ... it takes a lot more stamina and patience than I thought possible.... [T]he cold, hard reality is that in your first years of teaching, and maybe even after that, it's almost like you're slinging in the mud pits. Honestly, you get thrown to the wolves.... I know I'm going to stay in it because that's what I want to do, it's my resolve. But I can see why some people might be unsure.

3. Take a Strong, Positive Stance Toward Teaching

All our study participants reported success and fulfillment in their first three years of teaching, while being realistic about the difficulties. All showed awareness of how much their students learned and of their own professional worth, even where this was not acknowledged by outsiders. Liane in her second year said:

> [R]ight now, I think I'm doing the best English teaching I've done so far in my career.... I'm able to combine teaching literary elements with the major social issues that the [novel we're studying] deals with; and the kids are very much into it.

Jeannie, in year 3, commented: "I think I make a big difference, especially in a school like ours where a lot of the parents are on shift work and not necessarily spending a ton of time with their children."

4. Seek Help and Collaborate

In a large research study across several school districts, Lortie (1975) found that teachers "turn to one another for assistance and consider such peer help their most important source of assistance" (p. 76). Seeing yourself as going to others for help, learning from them, and collaborating with them are important aspects of your identity as a teacher. These themes emerged often in our study of new teachers.

a. Getting Help From Other Teachers

A large proportion of our study participants stressed the importance of going to other teachers for help. Heather proposed saying to new teachers:

> Talk to as many experienced teachers as possible, because the teachers in the school have so many resources.... If you're teaching primary, try to talk to the primary teachers ... nobody has everything but you can get a bit from here and there.... And those things are all tested, that's the good thing ... they have already used them in their own classroom.

b. Learning From and With Other Teachers

Paul felt that looking to other teachers for help was important not just for beginners but for all teachers:

> A key thing for a new teacher – well, any teacher – is to get out there and talk to other teachers. You get tired and stressed and just feel like holing up in your room … but that's the worst thing you can do.

Similarly, Tanya suggested that teachers will always need to be asking questions of their colleagues:

> I talked to one teacher around the corner who is retiring, and I asked her, "How do you do that?" and she said, "Oh, it's hard. It's just hard." And it's interesting to talk to someone who's been in the profession for 30 years and who's saying, "Yes, it's a challenge, and yes, I still ask that question too, and we're doing the best we can, and this is the way I do it."

c. Collaborating With Other Teachers

Apart from learning from others, many of the interviewees saw the need for regular collaboration with other teachers, whether in pairs, in teams, or at a whole-school level. Wanda said that if you have "a cohesive team and a team approach, then it makes it a lot easier for the students. They know what to expect going forward."

5. Look After Yourself

As a teacher, you also need to pay attention to your *own* well-being if you are to:

- survive;
- have the energy to help your students in the long-term;
- model a sound way of life for your students;
- give helpful input in classroom discussion of life issues.

Many of the new teachers we studied thought it essential to attend to their own needs, despite their hectic work schedule.

a. Life–Work Balance

This was a common theme. John said he would advise new teachers to take time for themselves, find people who can support them, and "practice what they preach" about balanced living. Marisa, at the end of her third year, talked about how she was finally achieving a better "home–work balance":

> I'm getting better at it. I've given myself more permission, especially in the last couple of months, to watch TV at 9:00 at night if I want to, rather than planning until 10:30 as I did in the first couple of years. And I'm realizing that things will be okay tomorrow if I don't spend that extra half-hour planning. That comes partly from experience: getting better at seeing what needs to be done and how long it will take.

b. Sustainability

Sustainability was also emphasized. Paul in his first year noted that "teaching is like any profession where you're giving yourself, so to speak, and have to make sure you're not giving yourself away too quickly. It has to be sustainable." At the end of his third year (in which he had a very difficult special needs class), he reported:

> Because my class was especially hard [this year], I learned by February not to think about it when I left the building.... I knew the only way I was going to get through the year was to go home and totally forget about it.... [C]ompared with previous years, I really had a weekend, I really had an evening, I went home and didn't think about stuff.

c. Not Beating Up On Yourself

This, or expecting too much of yourself, was mentioned by many. Karen observed that mistakes are a natural part of the learning process:

> Second-year teaching is still hard, but I'm trying to think of myself as a work in progress. I'm learning new things every day, and not expecting to do things perfectly.... And I think it's a positive attitude because the kids are also learning new things every day. And if they make comments about my not doing something perfectly, or making a mistake, I bring it back to that's how learning is, we all make mistakes and still have things to learn.

d. Improving Your Practice Gradually

Many advocated making things manageable by implementing just one or two innovations at a time. Sophia, in her third year, said:

I came out of teachers college ... wanting to do it all. But I now realize that I'm building my program a bit at a time: I can't do it all in one year.... I have these visions, but each year I play with it and mix it up a bit.... I do the best I can.

6. Grow Professionally

All the new teachers in our study spoke in varying degrees about the value of professional development to increase effectiveness and to make teaching more fulfilling. For example, Jody said: "You always have to learn. My education is not finished, it's ongoing. Even if I was teaching grade 1 every year, it's an ongoing thing. Professional development is so important." The PD included:

- professional reading, workshops, and courses;
- professional learning in one's own school and classroom.

7. Develop a Sense of Career Trajectory

Lortie (1975) points out that, "[c]ompared with most other kinds of middle-class work, teaching is relatively 'career-less.' There is less opportunity for the movement upward which is the essence of career" (p. 84). The status of a new, young teacher "is not appreciably different from that of the highly experienced old-timer" (p. 85).

Until this situation changes, much depends on you as a teacher taking the initiative and fashioning a career path for yourself. For example:

- becoming an increasingly strong and well-informed teacher;
- becoming a "lead teacher" or "resource teacher" in your school;
- becoming an educational writer while still teaching (like Vivian Paley or Nancie Atwell);
- doing part-time pre-service or in-service teaching (which may later become full-time);
- becoming a principal who to a significant degree is a curriculum leader in the school;
- starting an alternative school of some sort (e.g., private school, charter school).

Many of the new teachers in our study already had ideas about potential career trajectories for themselves. For example, John, in his second year, commented:

[In the future, I will] largely continue what I'm doing, enjoying that I'm a teacher, teaching grade 3.... Progressively, however, I would like to ... go back and get my master's ... and maybe start moving around a bit, teaching grade 1 and eventually grade 6.... And I would be interested in moving towards teaching at a school of education one day.

Marisa, in her second year, spoke mainly about working to fill gaps in her math pedagogy and long-range planning. By her third year, however, she was looking further ahead:

The more I teach, the more I realize that I love teaching language – reading, writing, and so on. And I enjoy working with my ESL students as well. So I'm thinking about maybe in the future teaching ESL or even working as a teacher librarian. But I'd have to do my qualifications, so those are more long-term goals.

Felicity, at the end of her third year, had rather firm ideas about her future, especially what would *not* be appropriate for her:

I went back to school as a mature student [and] I don't think I could actually survive twenty years in a classroom. I don't mean that in a negative way, but it really is so tiring ... and I don't want to be in the classroom if I'm exhausted and crabby.... I thought a bit about administration, but if you think teaching is hard, you really have to be a special person to go into administration. So I'm thinking rather of curriculum development or teacher education, down the road.

ACTIVITY: During Practice Teaching

- How has your view of the role of the teacher changed now that you are in the classroom?
- What part(s) of the role of the teacher do you find most demanding?
- Which of your hobbies and interests could you incorporate into your work as a teacher? Ask your cooperating teacher if you could share some of these with your students.
- Talk to your cooperating teachers about the kind of support they had as beginning teachers. Ask them to tell you about the induction support available in their school districts.
- Keep track of the number of hours you spend teaching, marking, and preparing your lessons. Is the workload manageable? If not, how can you go about reducing it?
- Ask your cooperating teachers about their on-going professional development. Do they recommend any particular conferences?

- Think about one improvement you made in your teaching and pat yourself on the back. Then think about one improvement you would like to make in your first year of teaching.
- Attend a faculty meeting to get a sense of how teachers and administrators work (or don't work) together.
- Be sure to eat lunch in the staff room/faculty lounge. Get to know the other teachers in your school. Try to feel like a member of the school community.

Conclusion

Your professional identity as a teacher is your overall perception of yourself as a professional. This self-perception must be quite broad. You need to understand that a wide array of tasks are involved in helping children succeed in school and in life, and you must willingly embrace this broad role. This does not mean you have to sacrifice yourself. On the contrary, adopting a broad approach to teaching can lead to greater professional success and satisfaction. Moreover, it is legitimate to approach teaching in a way that is personally feasible and helps you flourish as a human being. Only in this way will you be able to survive as a teacher, continue to be there for your students, and model a way of life that is instructive and inspiring to them.

As a pre-service student, you should work to understand and accept this broad role and achieve a sound integration of the personal and professional. You should learn about the extensive challenges of teaching, but explore how you can be effective and fulfilled despite these challenges. You need to embark on a path of continued professional growth, taking advantage of formal in-service programs but also opportunities to learn in your own classroom and school.

Chapter 7

A Vision for Teaching

Having a "philosophy" or general teaching approach – what many today call a "vision" – is another key element in teaching. It pulls together the other components, providing an overview and integration of them. When a teacher or school has a well-developed vision that meets the needs of all members of the community, there is a sense that we are all pulling in the same direction. However, developing a vision is a complicated task.

PERSONAL ACTIVITY

Have you ever been part of a group or organization that had a vision, a philosophy, or a certain way of being (e.g., religious community, sports group, social community)? What was the vision? How was it conveyed to new members? In what ways did the vision help and/or hinder the community? The individual? Briefly summarize your vision for teaching.

Why is Having a Vision for Teaching Important?

1. A vision keeps you aware of the wide range of goals and processes of teaching.
2. A vision helps you connect the various elements in teaching.
3. Having a vision enables you to explain to your students the purpose of learning activities.
4. Having a vision helps you explain your teaching approach not only to your students but to your students' parents, your colleagues, friends, relatives, hiring committees, and so on.

The new teachers in our study saw the value of having a teaching philosophy or vision. Sophia reported that "what my teacher education program did for me was help foster my philosophy, and my philosophy is what makes me the teacher I am: it is more important than any learning activity they taught me." Tanya commented:

> There is no way [the pre-service faculty] could have taught everything we needed from September to June for every grade level and every situation. But I think they gave us the philosophy we needed to make our way through our first year.

When the new teachers were critical of this aspect of the pre-service program, it was not because they thought a philosophy or vision was unimportant but because it was not explained clearly enough or with sufficient indication of its practical implications.

What is a Vision for Teaching?

The term "vision" may suggest something very general or even "other-worldly." But today – in education – it increasingly refers to a comprehensive set of principles and images of practice that guide a teacher (Grossman et al., 2000; Hammerness, 2006). Kennedy (2006) says:

> Although I use the term *vision* to describe teachers' plans, I do not mean this in the religious, idealist, or head-in-the-clouds sense of the term but rather, to mean that teachers have a feet-on-the-ground sense of purpose and direction and of actions that get there from here. They are plans ... scenarios that are envisioned.
>
> (p. 207)

As noted above, such "envisioned plans" are sometimes called a "philosophy" or "approach," and these terms have merit. But the word "vision" has important additional connotations: it suggests components such as vivid images of practice and emotional commitment by the teacher (Hammerness, 2006). A vision is more obviously something a teacher can be passionate about. Nevertheless, *you should not feel you have to use this particular word*: what matters is that you have something like a vision, whatever word you use.

While having a vision for teaching is useful in pointing you in promising directions, your vision should remain flexible and changeable. It should always be seen as a work in progress, open to modification in light of your ongoing experience and learning.

Marisa's Vision for Teaching: A Case Study

> You must have clear goals, you must know where you're going, and you build your lessons on that. I think that's what adds to my stress

because I spend so much time planning my lessons, and planning where I'm going to go. It's not just the day before, with me thinking, "Okay, what am I going to do tomorrow?" I try to link things as much as possible.

Background

Marisa is an extremely talented young teacher. Since obtaining her teaching credential, she has taught grades 4, 5, and combined 4/5 in the same urban school, with about 50 percent English Language Learners. Most of the ELL students are recent immigrants from Somalia, Ethiopia, Korea, and Eastern Europe. There are some middle-class families in the neighborhood but the school is classified as high needs. Marisa speaks highly of her initial undergraduate degree, a four-year program in Early Childhood Education (infancy through the primary grades) with a strong emphasis on child development and field placements each year. She then attended a two-year teacher credential program at OISE/UT. Although she felt the practicum placements in the latter program did not provide examples of good literacy instruction ("the programs did not have a focus"), she found the university literacy courses valuable. While completing her pre-service program, Marisa worked at summer camps, first as a counselor and later in a supervisory position.

For the classroom observations of our study participants, research team members are asked to provide four words they feel best characterize the teaching approach of the new teacher they are observing. One of the researchers described Marisa using the terms "scholarly," "routines," "group learning," and "respect/community," while another saw her as "thoughtful," "relational," "organized," and "teaching with a purpose." Yet these terms do not fully capture the essence of Marisa. When observing her, we were continually impressed by the construction of her lessons, each step clearly thought through, all done in a warm, supportive class community. She spends an extraordinary amount of time on lesson planning because she believes that lessons need to build on each other in line with a conception of where the program is headed.

Vision for her Literacy Program

In her third year of teaching, Marisa described her vision for literacy teaching as follows:

> I want to teach students a variety of strategies for reading a variety of texts. I want them to be able to talk about what they are reading and know that, for example, when you're reading non-fiction there are several components to it. I want them to know the proper terms

and be able to talk about them, explain how they are used, and use them. I want them to enjoy reading but I also want them to talk about books and really understand them. In terms of writing, I hope they will see writing as something they can have fun with. I know I wasn't raised that way. I want them to see writing as something that is free, you can choose whatever writing form you want, you can express ideas, it's up to you.

Marisa's vision may be elaborated in terms of four aspects of her work.

1. Sequencing the Program

Marisa feels that one of the challenges of teaching is knowing when to teach a particular topic or concept, and she believes she must choose the order of topics and skills based on the research on how children learn. When teaching mathematics she knows that you must teach skip counting before multiplication, yet she feels there is not the same certainty regarding literacy. Working with her mentor, grade team, and in-school literacy coordinator, Marisa has developed a well-sequenced program. She refers to the research literature and continually tries to balance short-term and long-term goals. She said:

> I am not teaching character traits just because it's fun and that's all I can think of, I am teaching them because next we're going to be focusing on relating to text. It will help kids relate to text better if they can identify and relate to the characters.

She has developed an approach to planning that works for her, conceptualizing her program in six-week blocks: three weeks of reading (e.g., workshop, whole-group instruction, individual reading) followed by three weeks of writing (e.g., workshop, modeled writing, individual and group projects). She has found this system highly effective because it links reading and writing, and provides students with sufficient exposure to a concept, genre, or skill before having to incorporate it in their writing. For example, when doing a newspaper unit, she spent a few weeks having the children read and study newspapers, "looking at bias, fact versus opinions, and how newspapers are supposed to be based on facts." After this intensive study, the students produced a class newspaper.

2. Engaging the Students

Marisa uses a range of teaching techniques and develops interesting end-of-unit projects for students to demonstrate their learning. She carefully chooses topics from the mandated curriculum that are relevant and interesting. For example, she has a poem of the week, word walls for content areas, and debates on topics such as, "Have cell phones improved our lives?" And she has the class read topical novels such as *The Breadwinners* (there are a number of Muslim students in her class, several of them from Afghanistan). She is well aware that many of her students do not have the same opportunities that children from more advantaged families may have. She addresses this by using videos, going on field trips, incorporating non-fiction texts in the program, and sharing her life experiences with the students:

> They need background knowledge. A reluctant reader or even a struggling reader, if they know a lot about a topic, that will help them understand what they are reading. And so I hope to build that background knowledge and expose them to things that are happening in the world as well.

3. Being Selective and Teaching Skills for Life-Long Learning

One of the struggles Marisa faces with program planning is the sheer volume of content to be covered. By the end of her first year of teaching, she already realized that she could not address all the official expectations:

> I'm starting to learn that, as someone said to me once, there are no curriculum police and no one is really going to know if I teach all the expectations. Anyway, it's unrealistic to assume – especially in a content area – that you can cover everything. And why would I want to?

She does not want to simply "cover the curriculum"; rather, she aims to teach skills, ones that students can apply in their own reading and writing and that will stay with them. In her third year, she said:

> I'm getting better at choosing what's important. That's debatable, because what one person thinks is important another person might have a different opinion about. What I try to do is focus on the skills involved, the bigger concepts, and not just the facts, particularly in science and social studies. I know they will forget the facts a few years from now. I try to use science and social studies as a vehicle to teach skills, like making observations, applying what you know to the outside world, and building background knowledge.

Whenever possible, she makes links with the students' lives, teaching skills they can use beyond the classroom. For example:

> a lot of our kids love being on the Internet, they are very adept at surfing the Net, and they're motivated. But they need to be taught how to use it effectively in terms of doing research. Or they need to be taught how to use it safely or critically.

She incorporates these skills into her content area teaching; for example, which search engines help you when researching a specific topic such as popular music.

4. Building a Strong Community

One of the foundational pieces of Marisa's vision is for the class to become a learning community. Her success in achieving this is evident in the way the children talk to each other and work together. She uses many of the strategies she learned in the Tribes training she completed while a student teacher. She talks to the students about their community, helping them acquire the necessary language and grasp the importance of social skills. She believes that by having a collaborative culture in the class she is able to use many more teaching techniques (e.g., group-work, Readers' Theater, debates). She incorporates learning about community into her literacy program.

> A lot of the books for read-alouds were about community. There were books about different kinds of families, different roles, boys versus girls, and issues we dealt with in class. Every time we read a different book, we would talk about, "Okay, what can we learn about building community from this book?" And the kids brainstormed things like "friends should support each other," and "everyone is equal, regardless of the color of their skin."

Marisa's Class in Action

Marisa's classroom reflects a language-rich environment, with bins of books, word walls, charts, posters, and student work on display. The classroom is old but very tidy and inviting. When Marisa's grade 4 and 5 students enter the class, there is a friendly buzz. They gather on the carpet by the whiteboard to review the characters in the book *Dionella* (a fractured fairy tale). They have been working on different genres of literature and are now studying fairy tales. Marisa forms random groups and each must identify three character traits of a particular character in *Dionella*.

After about 15 minutes, she uses a rain stick to get the students' attention to reconvene on the carpet. She has copied some dialogue from the book on charts, and the students who discussed a particular character have to read the lines in a way that reveals their character. There is lots of laughter and enthusiasm for the task. Marisa uses sophisticated language such as "Add a little more arrogance to your voice" as she gives feedback to the students. The students then work in groups (previously selected by Marisa) to practice their Readers' Theater (based on the same fairy tale) that they will perform later in the week. Again, the groups work very well together, with students assisting each other with the text (the ELL students are mixed into the groups and the grade 4 and 5 students work together).

After recess, the class meets on the carpet for a math lesson. They begin by working with a partner to practice their multiplication facts. After the drill, they have a lesson on doubling (multiplication). Students are attentive and keen. After each student gives his or her answer, Marisa asks for an explanation of the pattern. The students are used to explaining their answers and use correct mathematical language. She then distributes mini-whiteboards and the whole class practices doubling patterns. As the end of the day approaches, the students tidy up and organize their homework. Throughout the day, the environment in the class has been calm and friendly. It is obvious that the children enjoy school and are happy in the class.

Final Thoughts

Marisa's vision for teaching was shaped by many factors: her own love of reading and writing, her strong undergraduate program, the emphasis on research in her teacher credential program, the fine mentoring she received, the principal of the school who is very knowledgeable about literacy teaching, her reading of professional texts, and her induction workshops. She is proud of her program and rightly so. She said she would give the following advice to a new teacher:

> Don't be overwhelmed by all of the resources out there … because you can get too caught up with doing things that are fun and having neat lessons. If it doesn't connect back to your overall planning, your overall expectations, and if it doesn't make sense in the sequence of your whole year, then you're wasting your time.

CASE STUDY ACTIVITY: In small groups, discuss the case study generally, then consider the following questions.

- Marisa's vision for her class was shaped by many factors. What factors have influenced your vision for teaching?
- Marisa outlined her vision for literacy. List some of the subjects you may be required to teach. Under each, list five-to-seven broad goals that would guide your work. As you do so, keep in mind the two challenges – enactment and complexity – described in the Introduction.
- Marisa is very thoughtful about developing and sequencing her program; however, beginning teachers often find this part of program planning difficult. Discuss why it is difficult to figure out the sequence of your program. Identify ways of improving your skills of sequencing topics and assessments.
- What are the links between program planning (Chapter 1) and vision for teaching?

Problems of Developing a Vision for Teaching

While it is important for you to have a teaching vision, there are a number of potential challenges in developing one.

1. The visions presented in books and courses are often too abstract.
2. Some visions for teaching are too narrow. (The focus in schooling is often on transmitting "school knowledge," with little attention to the needs of work, citizenship, and personal and social growth.)
3. Visions are often unrealistic.
4. Some visions are too fragmented.
5. A teacher's vision is often seen as just a matter of opinion, not something to inquire into and discuss.

Key Elements of a Vision for Teaching

In this section, we discuss a number of elements or components that we think are vital to a sound vision for teaching. As in previous chapters, we draw on the views and practices of the new teachers in our study, along with other sources. The components highlighted have already been mentioned at earlier points in the book. We summarize them briefly here – with new quotations from the teachers in our study – to help you in exploring the nature and role of a vision for teaching.

A vision for teaching is much more than a vision or mission statement. It is a *vast network* of ideas, principles, and images touching on both theory and practice. The elements outlined below represent just a small proportion of a teaching vision, and are used mainly to *illustrate* what a vision is. However, in our view, these are very important elements that are frequently neglected in schooling. Reviewing them serves to show how having – or not having – a vision can make a great deal of difference.

Underlying these components are a handful of even more basic principles, notably: an inquiry approach to education; student construction of knowledge; interactive teaching; and individualization of teaching. We will often refer to these basic principles in our discussion since they are essential to our vision for teaching; however, they will not be our main focus here because we wish to work at a more concrete level.

The sample elements of our vision for teaching are:

1. pursuing a broad range of goals;
2. selecting and prioritizing objectives, topics, and activities;
3. connecting to students' lives;
4. engaging students;
5. teaching for depth;
6. integrating learning;
7. building community in the classroom;
8. teaching inclusively;
9. getting to know your students well.

ACTIVITY: During the Academic Program

Review the nine elements in the box on this page. Consider the following questions.
- How important is each element in a vision for teaching?
- Should some of them be deleted from your "high priority" list? Should others be added?
- How important is it to make such elements *explicit*, to yourself and others?

In small groups, discuss the functions that schools perform in society. List them on a chart paper. Each person should now go through the list and rank what she or he believes to be the top-three functions (functions schools *should* provide). Beside each of your three points, identify ways that the school or teacher can help realize this function. As a group, discuss the different rankings. Are there any commonalities among your lists?

1. Pursuing a Broad Range of Goals

A narrow vision will confine your approach to teaching and not allow you to pursue a multiplicity of purposes for your students. The purposes include not only subject knowledge and general cognitive development but also social, emotional, aesthetic, moral, behavioral, and other forms of growth. Schooling today in many countries takes up a great deal of young people's lives – 12, 14, or even 18 years (if we include kindergarten and undergraduate university). In many ways, schooling *is* their life for one-fifth to one-quarter of their time on the planet. Among the new teachers in our study, Karen said:

> I want to have fun and I want the kids to have fun too. It's important that they're not just learning facts but learning social skills, how to treat each other, how to talk about their feelings … and developing empathy. That's more important than just facts.

Paul commented:

> Having good social relationships is really important, and if kids leave my class with a good sense of citizenship, responsibility, and independence, knowing how to get along with people, taking pride in their work, that is what I want. I want them to learn reading strategies too, but they can only learn them if they have the right attitudes to approach them.

2. Selecting and Prioritizing Objectives, Topics, and Activities

While you need a broad set of goals, you should not try to cover everything. You must select and prioritize goals, topics studied, and learning activities. Some goals are more important than others; and besides, no matter how worthy various goals are, if you cover too much your teaching will be superficial. Teachers are under a great deal of pressure today to teach every part of an extremely detailed official curriculum. To fulfill your employment mandate, it may be necessary to *touch on* a great many topics; but you should make choices about which topics to address thoroughly. As John commented:

> With my class this year, their reading was very strong but their writing was a big concern, so I focused a lot more on writing.... Is that appropriate? I think so, because if something is lacking, why should you spread your time across everything?... A strength of a teacher is to be able to allocate different timelines to what needs to be covered.

In her third year, Wanda reported: "I'm more concerned [now] about making sure the kids have a solid knowledge base in each of the subject areas, rather than hitting all 250 or 300 specific curriculum expectations."

3. Connecting to Students' Lives

Among the goals in a sound teaching vision are ones that relate to students' way of life: present and future, in the school and beyond. Schooling must be of use to students in a broad sense that includes not only their career but many other aspects of life as well. Moreover, if students are to connect school learning to life, they must become self-conscious about developing *a way of life*. Too often, young people (and adults, for that matter) see their way of life as a given, rather than something they can create or at least fine-tune. A major aspect of your vision for teaching should be supporting students in consciously building a way of life.

Many of our study participants stressed the need to connect to students' everyday lives, both present and future. Sophia reported that, although in a sense she prepares students for standardized tests, her main concern is to give them "strategies for life ... strategies they will not only be using for test writing but also in life, to figure out solutions to problems." Carrie noted: "I talk a lot about what adults do in different jobs [and relate it to their studies]: why would you need to know how to do this? Why is it important?"

4. Engaging Students

Students will not always enjoy their learning, even when they can see its importance. But the high degree of alienation from school work often found among students today is unacceptable. You should try to bring students on-board by giving them more choice and systematically explaining the value of what they are studying. Often, you will need to individualize instruction. While individualizing teaching is challenging, it is necessary in many instances.

The new teachers in our research emphasized the need to engage students. Wanda stressed getting to know students so you can choose appropriate books for them and find "the big hook that's going to draw the child in. Because if the child is not engaged they're not going to learn, they'll just turn you off." Paul said:

> The first thing I want to do is get the students excited and interested. Because although some of them have specific needs or disabilities, for the most part they just need to get connected to something they're really excited about. So for some students, letting them read

something that maybe isn't at their grade level but that they're interested in – a newspaper, something on the Internet, a recipe book, or whatever – will get them reading.

5. Teaching for Depth

As discussed in Chapter 5, subject-matter learning is very important. However, it is only valuable if it goes beyond superficial memorization of "facts" to grasping key concepts and issues in depth. Many aspects of the vision for teaching noted so far relate to this point. For example:

* selecting and prioritizing are necessary so that you can focus in-depth on a smaller number of crucial topics;
* engaging students and connecting to their lives lead to their inquiring into topics more deeply and understanding them more fully.

Many of the new teachers we were studying spoke of the need to teach in-depth. For example, Anita reported that her goal in literacy teaching is: "to have the kids be able to understand what they're reading, talk about it, think about it critically, and then express their thoughts ... in a clear, organized way so other people can read them."

Liane noted:

A concern I've had about my program in the past is not having time to go deeply into anything. I've felt I'm just touching on things: floating around and not achieving anything great. So this year I really slowed down. I wanted to spend a lot of time making it great: working on introductions, arguments, how to conclude.... [A]nd it paid off; some of their essays were fabulous.

6. Integrating Learning

Integration of learning is another important aspect of a vision for teaching.

* Integrating subjects and topics helps engage students: they see what they are learning in context, rather than as just one more thing to cover. This in turn fosters inquiry and knowledge construction by students.
* Integration makes learning deeper as students grasp the underlying principles and the connections between subjects.
* Integration enables you to address many different topics at once, thus providing more time to pursue issues in depth.

- Integrated learning is more authentic and useful because in the "real world" most problems cut across discipline lines.
- Integration enables you to teach in a more holistic manner since you deal with cognitive, social, and emotional learning together, e.g., literature and the arts, history and literature, science and politics.

According to Anita, the learning of spelling and grammar should be integrated into broader literacy activities rather than being dealt with separately:

[T]he key thing is to not just talk about [a word or grammar rule] once but rather to show its importance by bringing it up again and again ... showing its value by modeling and making it stand out. That way they tend to remember it.

Sophia reported:

I try to integrate math with other subjects. Right now I'm doing probability in math, and I link that with prediction in reading, because probability is about being able to predict what's going to happen next.... And we're also doing medieval times at present, and I connect work on historical timelines with the study of math and time.

7. Building Community in the Classroom

Building a strong class community – with the teacher as a member – should be central to your teaching vision. Class community

- supports the *social* construction of knowledge, increasingly emphasized today (Beck & Kosnik, 2006; Richardson, 1997);
- helps achieve some of the broader goals of teaching, such as acquiring social skills and understanding human nature and interactions;
- links the classroom to the "multiliteracies" of the outside world as students share aspects of their home and local community life;
- leads to more engagement in inquiry: because students know each other, they are more willing to participate and say what they think in small groups and whole-class settings;
- reduces classroom management problems, thus leaving more time for in-depth teaching.

Building community in the classroom was a major aspect of the vision for teaching articulated by the new teachers in our study. For example, Maria said:

[K]ids often don't know how to have a conversation.... Since the first day of school, I've been drilling them about manners, even just when someone greets you, "Hi, how are you today?" you ask the person back, "I'm fine thanks, how are you?"

Tanya commented:

I've worked hard on having a very helpful [classroom] environment, and especially having the students help each other. We've done a lot of talking about, okay, you have a problem, before you come to me what are you going to do to try to solve it? The main goal is cooperation and class community.

8. Teaching Inclusively

Taking account of the diverse backgrounds and abilities of students is essential to connecting to their lives, engaging them, building class community, and many other aspects of the teacher's role. You should not view teaching inclusively as a frill or the politically correct thing to do, but as a fundamental dimension of sound teaching. Inclusion is inherent in a teaching approach that respects students' circumstances, talents, and experiences, and seeks to enlist them in constructing knowledge.

Turning to the views of our new teachers, Sophia stressed attending to "the different cultures and background experiences of all the students." John spoke about the need to "tailor [your program] to the students you're teaching," and gave an example:

[W]e made a quilt.... Not a lot of kids in my class celebrate Christmas, so I said "Well, for each square of this quilt, I want you to write about a special occasion in your religion for the year." So a lot of the kids wrote about Chinese New Year, a lot about Eids, that type of thing as well as Christmas. So I was able to bring us all together to hold hands as a group, I guess, and put it together on a quilt that I've hung outside my classroom.

9. Getting to Know Your Students Well

Getting to know your students is basic to all other aspects of a sound vision for teaching. Pursuing diverse goals, prioritizing topics and activities, engaging students, teaching for depth, and integrating learning depend on the teacher knowing students' individual interests, abilities, and needs. Community building and inclusion require you to model a caring, respectful relationship with each student. Connecting to students' lives is such a sensitive task that it is not feasible unless you know your students well and have a positive rapport with them.

Among the new teachers in our study, Anna commented:

> [W]here I've connected most with the students is just the chats, their coming to me when they have a problem. Not necessarily academic – though they like the way I explain things to them several times and so on. But it's more how I connect to them. They feel I'm not just an adult in the classroom but somebody they can talk to.

Vera, looking back at the end of her third year, said:

> I don't think my ideals have changed ... but I do find myself enjoying the kids' company a lot more. In my first year, I was mainly concerned about keeping them busy, and now my concern is more talking to them, getting to know them, learning about how they learn, and then using that to teach them.

ACTIVITY: During Practice Teaching

- Look around your classroom. What is on the walls? What does the classroom (e.g., layout, materials posted on bulletin boards) say about the teacher's vision?
- What would you want outside visitors to say about your work as a teacher? From their observation, what would they say about your vision for teaching?
- Think about your cooperating teacher's program in its entirety. How does it reveal their vision? How well does it match the principles outlined earlier in the box. How well does it match your vision?
- Think about some of the lessons you have taught. Which ones do you think are helping your students in their life *beyond* the school? Which ones are only fulfilling a narrow band of skills? Which ones did you enjoy teaching?
- Think about conversations you have had with your students over the past few days. How much time did you spend talking to the students about their life *outside* school? How well do you feel that you know your students? Which students do you feel you do not know well? Why?
- Which of your lessons were "in sync" with your vision for schooling?
- How is your vision changing from the one you developed during your apprenticeship of observation, as explained in the Introduction?

ACTIVITY: Resource Kit

If a student, associate teacher, or parent gives you a card or note with positive feedback or praise, put it in your Resource Kit. You might want to start a file called "Kudos" or "Positive Feedback" or "Why I Went Into Teaching." Continue to add cards and notes; at regular intervals, read them to remind yourself about the difference you are making in the lives of your students.

Conclusion

In order to make sound decisions about what and how to teach, you need a comprehensive, integrated understanding of the goals, principles, and practices of teaching. Because of its distinctive connotations, the word "vision" is increasingly used to refer to this understanding. But the particular term is not crucial: it could equally be called a "philosophy" or "theory of teaching" or an "approach to teaching." The main point is that it integrates all the other priorities, shows what they mean in practice, and keeps you aware of the enormous range of considerations involved in teaching, including the many links to everyday life and the "real world."

Without a vision, gathering endless strategies, practical tips, and curriculum information will not help you much as a teacher. You need a broad, integrated set of goals, priorities, and principles. However, your vision must be concrete as well as theoretical. Throughout your career, you need to keep adding new areas to your theory and practice and seeing more connections between the elements. You can do this through:

- reading professional books and articles;
- attending workshops and courses;
- experimenting;
- discussing with colleagues;
- thinking about your practice;
- seeking feedback from your students;
- learning more about the world through movies, TV, the Internet, plays, novels, non-fiction reading, newspapers, travel, socializing, talking to students, colleagues, parents, and so on.

References

Ainscow, M., Booth, T., & Dyson, A. (2006). *Improving schools, developing inclusion*. London: Routledge.

Allington, R. (2006). *What really matters for struggling readers: Designing research-based programs* (2nd ed.). Boston: Pearson/Allyn & Bacon.

Atwell, N. (1998). *In the middle* (2nd ed.). Portsmouth: Heinemann.

Bainbridge, J., & Malicky, G. (2004). *Constructing meaning: Balancing elementary language arts* (3rd ed.). Toronto: Thomson/Nelson.

Ball, D. (2000). Bridging practices: Intertwining content and pedagogy in teaching and learning to teach. *Journal of Teacher Education, 51*(3), 241–247.

Ball, D., Thames, M., & Phelps, G. (2008). Content knowledge for teaching: What makes it special? *Journal of Teacher Education, 59*(5), 389–407.

Barone, D., & Morrow, L.M. (eds.) (2003). *Literacy and young children: Research-based practices*. New York: Guilford Press.

Barth, R. (1990). *Improving schools from within*. San Francisco: Jossey-Bass.

Beck, C., & Kosnik, C. (2006). *Innovations in teacher education: A social constructivist approach*. Albany: SUNY Press.

Clayton, C. (2007). Curriculum making as novice professional development: Practical risk taking as learning in high-stakes times. *Journal of Teacher Education, 58*(3), 216–230.

Connelly, M., & Clandinin, J. (1999). *Shaping a professional identity: Stories of educational practice*. New York: Teachers College Press.

Cossey, R., & Tucher, P. (2005). Teaching to collaborate, collaborating to teach. In L. Kroll, R. Cossey, D. Donahue, T. Calguera, V. LaBoskey, A. Richert, & P. Tucher (eds.), *Teaching as principled practice: Managing complexity for social justice* (pp. 105–120). Thousand Oaks: Sage.

Cunningham, P., & Allington, R. (2007). *Classrooms that work: They can all read and write* (4th ed.). Boston: Pearson/Allyn & Bacon.

Darling-Hammond, L. (1997). *The right to learn*. San Francisco: Jossey-Bass.

Darling-Hammond, L. (2006). *Powerful teacher education: Lessons from exemplary programs*. San Francisco: Jossey-Bass.

Darling-Hammond, L., Ancess, J., & Falk, B. (1995). *Authentic assessment in action: Studies of schools and students at work*. New York: Teachers College Press.

Darling-Hammond, L., Banks, J., Zumwalt, K., Gomez, L., Sherin, M., Griesdorn, J., & Finn, L. (2005). Educational goals and purposes. In L.

Darling-Hammond & J. Bransford (eds.), *Preparing teachers for a changing world: What teachers should learn and be able to do* (pp. 169–200). San Francisco: Jossey-Bass.

Dewey, J. (1938). *Experience and education.* New York: Collier-Macmillan.

Evertson, C., Emmer, E., & Worsham, M. (2006). *Classroom management for elementary teachers.* Boston: Pearson.

Falk, B. (2000). *The heart of the matter: Using standards and assessment to learn.* Portsmouth: Heinemann.

Fountas, I., & Pinnell, G. (2001). *Guiding readers and writers: Teaching comprehension, genre, and content literacy.* Portsmouth: Heinemann.

Gibbs, J. (2000). *Tribes: A new way of learning and being together.* Sausalito: Center Source Systems.

Grossman, P., & Schoenfeld, A. (2005). Teaching subject matter. In L. Darling-Hammond & J. Bransford (eds.), *Preparing teachers for a changing world: What teachers should learn and be able to do* (pp. 201–231). San Francisco: Jossey-Bass.

Grossman, P., Valencia, S., Evans, K., Thompson, C., Martin, C., & Place, N. (2000). Transitions into teaching: Learning to teach writing in teacher education and beyond. *Journal of Literacy Research, 32*(4), 631–662.

Hagger, H., & McIntyre, D. (2006). *Learning teaching from teachers: Realizing the potential of school-based teacher education.* Maidenhead: Open University Press.

Hammerness, K. (2006). *Seeing through teachers' eyes: Professional ideals and classroom practices.* New York: Teachers College Press.

Jacklin, A., Griffiths, V., & Robinson, C. (2006). *Beginning primary teaching: Moving beyond survival.* Maidenhead: Open University Press.

Kennedy, M. (2005). *Inside teaching: How classroom life undermines reform.* Cambridge, MA: Harvard University Press.

Kennedy, M. (2006). Knowledge and vision in teaching. *Journal of Teacher Education, 57*(3), 205–211.

Kohn, A. (1999). *The schools our children deserve.* New York: Houghton Mifflin.

Kosnik, C. (1999). *Primary education: Goals, processes, and practices.* Ottawa: Legas.

Labaree, D. (2004). *The trouble with ed schools.* New Haven: Yale University Press.

LePage, P., Darling-Hammond, L., & Akar, H. (2005). Classroom management. In L. Darling-Hammond & J. Bransford (eds.), *Preparing teachers for a changing world: What teachers should learn and be able to do* (pp. 327–357). San Francisco: Jossey-Bass.

Lortie, D. (1975). *Schoolteacher: A sociological study.* Chicago: University of Chicago Press.

McDonald, J. (1992). *Teaching: Making sense of an uncertain craft.* New York: Teachers College Press.

Martin, J.R. (1992). *The schoolhome.* Cambridge, MA: Harvard University Press.

Meier, D. (1995). *The power of their ideas.* Boston: Beacon Press.

Noddings, N. (2005). *The challenge to care in schools: An alternative approach* (2nd ed.). New York: Teachers College Press.

Otero, V. (2006). Moving beyond the "get it or don't" conception of formative assessment. *Journal of Teacher Education, 57*(3), 247–255.

Paley, V. (1992). *You can't say you can't play.* Cambridge, MA: Harvard University Press.

Peterson, M., & Hittie, M. (2003). *Inclusive teaching: Creating effective schools for all learners.* Boston: Allyn & Bacon.

Peterson, R. (1992). *Life in a crowded place.* Portsmouth: Heinemann.

Richardson, V. (ed.) (1997). *Constructivist teacher education: Building a world of new understandings.* London: Falmer.

Shepard, L. (2001). The role of classroom assessment in teaching and learning. In V. Richardson (ed.), *Handbook of research on teaching* (4th ed.) (pp. 1066–1101). Washington, DC: American Educational Research Association.

Shepard, L., Hammerness, K., Darling-Hammond, L., & Rust, F. (2005). Assessment. In L. Darling-Hammond & J. Bransford (eds.), *Preparing teachers for a changing world: What teachers should learn and be able to do* (pp. 275–326). San Francisco: Jossey-Bass.

Shulman, L. (1986). Those who understand: Knowledge growth in teaching. *Educational Researcher, 15*(2), 4–14. (Also in *The wisdom of practice*, chapter 6, pp. 189–215.)

Shulman, L. (2004). *The wisdom of practice: Essays on teaching, learning, and learning to teach.* San Francisco: Jossey-Bass.

Sleeter, C. (2005). *Un-standardizing curriculum: Multicultural teaching in the standards-based classroom.* New York: Teachers College Press.

Verma, G., Bagley, C., & Jha, M. (eds.) (2007). *International perspectives on educational diversity and inclusion.* London: Routledge.

Wood, G. (1992). *Schools that work.* New York: Penguin/Plume.

Zemelman, S., Daniels, H., & Hyde, A. (1998). *Best practice.* Portsmouth: Heinemann.

Index